# 50
# SUCCESSFUL
# HARVARD
# APPLICATION
# ESSAYS

# 50 SUCCESSFUL HARVARD APPLICATION ESSAYS

**What Worked for Them Can Help You Get into the College of Your Choice**

## 2ND EDITION

*With Analysis by the Staff of* The Harvard Crimson

St. Martin's Griffin ☙ NEW YORK

www.stmartins.com

Library of Congress Cataloging-in-Publication Data

50 successful Harvard application essays : what worked for them can
help you get into the college of your choice.—2nd ed.
    p. cm.
  ISBN 0-312-34376-0
  EAN 978-0-312-34376-7
  1. College applications—Massachusetts—Boston. 2. Harvard University—Admission. 3. Exposition (Rhetoric). I. Title: Fifty successful Harvard application essays. II. Harvard Crimson.

LB2351.52.U6A13 2005
378.1'616'097446—dc22

                                                    2005046587

Second Edition: September 2005

10  9  8  7  6  5  4  3  2  1

# Contents

Acknowledgments     vii

Fifteen Steps to Success—That May or May Not Prove to
Be Surefire     ix

## Memorable Moments

"The Handyman's Special" by Timothy Josiah Morris Pertz     3

"Schofield-Bodt Reigns for a Year" by Daniel Schofield-Bodt     6

"To Freeze a Moment" by Katya Rosenblatt     10

"Banana" by Nathan W. Hill     13

"A Night Unforgotten" by Frederick Antwi     16

"A Lesson About Life" by Aaron Miller     19

"Running Thoughts" by Nikhil Kacker     22

"Playing the Giramel's Behind" by Eliot I. Hodges     25

"Truly Alive" by James Collins     27

"Checkmate" by Robert M. Stolper     30

## Influences

"Dandelion Dreams" by Emmeline Chuang     35

"*Lyubov* and *Viktoria*" by Viktoria Slavina     38

"A Great Influence" by Michelangelo V. D'Agostino     41

"Michael and Me" by Brian R. McElroy     44

"A Mixture" by Anjanette Marie Chan Tack     47

"Tears and Fears" by Meaghan Beattie     51

"Two Good Friends" by Paul S. Gutman     55

"The Beast" by Daniel Myung     58

"Between a Rock and Home Plate" by Mark K. Arimoto     61

"Learning to Fly" by Inés Pacheco     66

"My Mother's Books" by Pat Blanchfield     70

## Points of View

"On Diplomacy in Bright Nike Running Tights" by
Christopher M. Kirchhoff     77

"The Magic of Magic" by Harrison R. Greenbaum     82

"The End Is Where We Start From" by Evan Henry Jacobs ... 86

"Introducing Clark Kent and Willy Wonka" by Daniel G. Habib ... 89

"Vietnamese Soup" by Michaela N. de Lacaze ... 94

"History as Calculus" by Jesse Field ... 97

"Thoughts Behind a Steam-Coated Door" by Neha Mahajan ... 100

"Interview with Myself" by Wesley Oliver ... 104

"A Grateful Glance into Trash" by David Soloveichik ... 107

"Catharsis in Uncluttering" by Katherine Chan ... 110

## Songs of Experience

"Should I Jump?" by Timothy F. Sohn ... 117

"Grandma's Living Room" by Rosa Norton ... 120

"A Mountain School Perspective," anonymous ... 123

"One Hundred Pairs of Eyes" by Patricia M. Glynn ... 126

"The Lost Game" by Stephanie A. Stuart ... 129

"Warm Hearts and a Cold Gun" by James A. Colbert ... 132

"In the Waiting Room" by Carlin E. Wing ... 135

"My Responsibility" by David J. Bright ... 139

"Lessons" by G. Tyler O'Brien ... 142

"E Pluribus Unum" by Corey Rennell ... 145

## Molding Identity

"Religion Reconsidered" by Alexis Maule ... 151

"A Periodical Affair" by Karen Feng ... 154

"The Art of Penning" by Lan Zhou ... 157

"Myung!" by Myung! H. Joh ... 159

"A Railroad of Memories" by Masha Godina ... 162

"Mosaic" by Laure E. De Vulpillières ... 166

"Myself" by Jamie Smith ... 172

"Who Am I?" by Michael Cho ... 175

"My Name" by Uyen-Khanh Quang-Dang ... 178

# Acknowledgments

*The Harvard Crimson*, the daily student newspaper of Harvard University, is back with our latest attempt to help you attack the college admissions essay and come out a winner. We have taken the strongest essays of our first edition of *50 Successful Harvard Application Essays* and combined them with several new pieces to help you face the challenge of writing a well-written, introspective, and engaging college admissions essay.

As with the first edition, we sought to collect a variety of essays that represent a wide range of writing styles, themes, and viewpoints. From the culinary delights that emerge from blending cultures to the art of mastering magic tricks, we have tried to cover the gamut of interests and writing techniques of Harvard students. These essays were selected based on style, creativity, and choice of subject. Following each essay, there is an analysis by one of the *Crimson*'s editors that offers a perspective on what the essay aims to do, how it goes about achieving this goal, its strengths, and its weaknesses. With this analysis, our aim was, again, diversity. In all, over fifteen *Crimson* staff members—from all areas of the paper from business to news reporting—contributed reviews.

None of the contributors to this book—neither the authors of the essays nor the authors of the analyses—is an expert. They are a collection of people who have been through the process themselves and want to help you in crafting a great essay. In other words, you will find many voices, some of which contradict one another. Listen to the ones that most resonate with you.

There is no formula to this book, just as there is no formula to writing your college essay—of course, we offer you some tips to get you on the right path. Our hope is that somewhere within these pages you will find inspiration for your work. Ultimately, though, your essay must be your own, just as these essays are the personal efforts of their authors.

I would like to thank everyone who helped revise this *Crimson* classic: Rebecca O'Brien and Lauren Schuker, my project coordinators; our agent, Linda Mead, for her help in shaping this vision; Tom Mercer, our editor at St. Martin's Press; Matthew Granade, the author of the original edition; and last but not least, all of the authors who submitted their essays and the *Crimson* editors who helped analyze them.

Good luck!

—Erica K. Jalli
President, 131st guard of *The Harvard Crimson*

# Fifteen Steps to Success—That May or May Not Prove to Be Surefire

So you want to write a college admissions essay.

By now you have undoubtedly received a wide range of advice from a wide range of sources: guidance counselors urging you to start early, parents worried about your vocabulary level, English teachers stressing the importance of proper grammar.

At this point you have also probably come to the realization that there is no one foolproof method for writing a winning admissions essay. In fact, much of the advice you have probably been given—and which you will read in this book—will probably contradict itself. Example: "Take a risk. Write about something that will make your essay stand out," versus "Don't take any chances. The admissions committee is looking for a well-written, well-argued essay. You can do that without coloring outside the lines." Another example: "The personal statement is only one part of your application. Don't stress," versus "Revise. Revise. Revise. Proofread. Proofread. Proofread. Draft multiple versions. This is the most important piece of writing you will ever produce."

As you can already see, the whole process can be very confusing. Don't let this discourage you. The most truthful advice that can be offered is that there is no one way to write a successful admissions essay. The essay—in terms of both its content and the manner in which it is written—is like you: unique. You can write about your family trip to Niagara Falls or you can write about meeting the Dalai Lama. You can talk about what a perfect student, brother, friend, or all-around good guy you are, or you can write about the day you threw a temper tantrum after losing the state tennis finals. The beauty of the personal statement is that it is completely personal.

Still, we have pledged to help you, and help you we will, by way of the following steps to writing a good, solid, impressive admissions essay. Many of these tips resemble advice your high school English teacher would offer. Others are advice that you may have heard from sisters, brothers, and friends. Some of it might even sound like nagging. It's still worth it for us to repeat them and for you to listen to them.

Here goes:

1. *Think strategically.* Your essay is an opportunity to show a part of yourself that neither your test scores nor your grades can convey. There are many ways to go about doing this. You can emphasize your creative talent, or you can play up an extracurricular activity or hobby that is particularly important to you. You can discuss a formative moment or an aspect of your life that you feel has shaped you. If you devote the essay to rehashing what is already apparent in the rest of the application, you lose a valuable space for self-expression.

2. *Be reflective.* Speak from the heart. Explain what the experience means to you, rather than simply recounting the experience as it happened. This is what gives your application a human component and differentiates you from everyone else. It's important to show how you have changed and developed into the person you are today.

3. *Start early.* Give yourself enough time to brainstorm and then let drafts sit so you have more time to proofread. The more time you have, the more you can make the essay truly reflect who you are.

4. *Brainstorm ideas* with friends, family members, and teachers. While the personal statement is one of the most intimate parts of the application, it certainly can benefit from constructive criticism. Don't rule out any essay topic because it's not impressive enough, exciting enough, or unique enough. You may not realize just how important it was for you to hit the game's

winning shot, or how much your support helped a family member get through a life-threatening illness. Those who know you best can give you very effective feedback.

5. *Avoid clichés* in your writing and be original in your ideas. This rule applies for images within your writing as well as for the topic of the essay itself. Be aware that some ideas—winning the state football/soccer/gymnastics championship—have been done at least a thousand times before you. There's nothing inherently wrong with addressing the thrill of victory and the agony of defeat, but try to be more original. Be memorable.

6. *Steer away from gimmicks.* People have pulled them off, but to do it, you have to do it well. If you're a great cartoonist, send in those comic strips. Or if you are a wonderful poet, go for it. Don't attempt to invent something just to make your essay stand out. Be subtle and tactful, using an authentic voice and wit. Remember, execution is everything and mediocrity doesn't win.

7. *If you don't know what a word means, don't use it.* Remember the "K.I.S.S." rule: keep it simple, stupid. Make two or three points and finish up. Don't overwhelm your reader with extraneous details. Even if you do know what a long word means, a short word might just as well express what you're trying to say. The SATs are your chance to flex those verbal muscles, and there is nothing worse than misusing a word in an essay.

8. *Stay "on message."* Admissions officers will read your essay in less than a few minutes, so keep the scale of the story manageable. Use relevant and specific anecdotes to prove your point. Every word should say something new. Read through the essay several times and trim repetitive or nonfunctional sentences. Don't expect to express all the nuances and complexities of what the death of a loved one meant in less than five hundred words. Keep the scope of your essay appropriate to the length.

9. *Start strong.* As any good essayist will tell you, it's the beginning that counts most. Remember that your reader is trying to glean a sense of who you are, so try and grab the reader's attention from the beginning. Make it easy for them, make them want to read on, and you will be rewarded.

10. *Conclusions are important.* Many times, a beautifully written essay is weakened with a moral at the end of the story. Don't ruin a perfectly good essay by launching into broad, sweeping generalizations. If you find yourself thinking that a platitude is necessary to prove your point, start revising. Returning to your opening line in your ending sentence is a good way to tie it all together. Just as the introduction will set the tone for the essay, the conclusion must resonate with the reader.

11. *Don't take yourself too seriously.* Don't be afraid to be yourself. Use humor if you are a funny person. As long as it's tasteful, it can't hurt you to make your reader smile.

12. *Relax.*

13. *Proofread.*

14. *Proofread.*

15. *Proofread.*

# MEMORABLE MOMENTS

# "The Handyman's Special"

By Timothy Josiah Morris Pertz, who attended a medium-sized private school in Lawrenceville, New Jersey.

I made my first trip to Costa Rica when I was fifteen. I spent a summer living with a Costa Rican family in the capital city of San José and studying at a language school. I was eager to absorb as much of the culture as I possibly could, and so for dinner on my first night in the country I stuffed myself with the most popular traditional dish, *gallo pinto*, or rice and beans.

The next morning I woke up early and walked a few blocks to the Costa Rican Language and Dance Academy. I was placed in a class, and for the rest of the morning I studied Spanish verbs and phrases. We broke for lunch at noon, and as the school emptied out I stayed behind in class to finish up a grammar exercise. I hadn't eaten breakfast and was hungry for some more *gallo pinto*, but just as I was walking out the door to go to lunch I felt nature call.

I remembered seeing the women's bathroom as I came in, but I didn't see one for the men. I wandered the halls. I saw no men's bathroom. I became desperate. Still no men's bathroom. I looked left, then right, swallowed my pride and slipped into the ladies' room.

It was only meant for one person, but wasn't at all small. It had several beautiful antique fixtures, such as a claw-foot porcelain bathtub (with a pile of rusty hangers in it) and an old toilet with a gold-plated handle.

I sat down and did what I had forgotten one generally does after eating lots of beans. I finished up (remembering to throw the toilet paper in the wastebasket, as is done in Costa Rica to keep the pipes from clogging) and pulled the gold-plated handle. Nothing happened. Huh, that's funny. Tried again. Nothing. Sh*t.

For years my father worked as a maintenance man at a summer camp, and had a great deal of experience with plumbing. I, however, had been sheltered from the world of waste removal and had been too concerned with the high pursuit of academia to learn my father's art. It took being stuck in the ladies' bathroom of a strange school in a foreign country with a full, broken toilet to make me realize the error of my ways.

There was no one around; I could have just slipped back out and no one would have known I was the culprit. But I knew I would dishonor my father if I walked away (it wouldn't reflect too well on me as a person either), so I decided I would try my best to deal with the situation.

For the first time in my life, I opened up the cover at the back of the toilet. I studied the mechanism for a minute and realized that there needed to be something that would connect the handle to the plug that drains the water. I looked around the room, grabbed a hanger from the bathtub, twisted it into a straight piece of wire, attached one end to the stopper and one to the handle, and flushed. I heard the swishing sound of success as the contents of the toilet disappeared into never-never land.

That day I learned what my father already knew, that life calls for an understanding not only of lofty topics, but of more practical matters as well. Most importantly, I learned not to run away from sticky situations, but to deal with them with grace, persistence, and a sense of humor. This was the first in a series of realizations about the importance of public service at the most down-and-dirty levels, the beginning of a personal transformation that would lead to my returning to Costa Rica the next summer to revive a recycling program in the Monteverde Cloud Forest.

But that was a ways in the future. For the moment, I needed to eat and get back to class. With newfound confidence and sense of purpose, I ran to the restaurant across the street and gobbled down a big plate of beans.

## ANALYSIS

Pertz chooses a particularly sticky subject that quite easily could have left him knee-deep in, well, his own shit. But despite the sensitive topic and the masculine tendency to revert to childish bathroom humor, he manages to string together a cohesive narrative that evokes the sympathy of the reader—it is, after all, a situation most of us have experienced, and far fewer have written about—while providing a modicum of insight into the applicant.

The essay itself is strongest when describing Pertz's aggrandized triumph in the stall. Embracing the "show, don't tell" philosophy, the scene, crafted to read almost as though drafted for a television sitcom, plays out anticlimactically, as he triumphs over his own ignorance of the mundane. The writing is simple and flows naturally. No need to interject SAT words to describe basic human functions we are all familiar with. Using the word "sh*t," a word not likely found in many personal statements, requires a calculated risk. Here, it works on two levels, conveying the mess he's facing and his feelings about it. Though it presumably didn't, this lack of formality could have backfired with the wrong reader, and is rarely a chance worth taking, though if you've chosen such an off-the-wall topic, you might as well just push the envelope a little bit further.

While the essay overcomes those potential stumbling points, it is certainly uneven, and the introduction and conclusion both lack the anecdote's intrigue. The first sentence is far from gripping and fails to hint at the nature of the story to follow. A more shocking opening would have captured a reader's attention, rather than preparing him or her for a middle-school vacation recap. The paragraphs following the story's resolution are particularly heavy-handed, and fall back on cliché and overused fluff. The reference to Pertz's return to Costa Rica to kickstart a recycling program seems forced, a transparent effort to mention his community service project here. The concluding paragraph is solid, however, colorfully hinting at the lessons learned without resorting to a clumsy "moral of the story" comment.

—Timothy J. McGinn

# "Schofield-Bodt Reigns for a Year"

By Daniel Schofield-Bodt, who attended a large public high school in Shelton, Connecticut.

*The following essay was submitted as a scanned document intended to look like a newspaper layout, with two text columns wrapped around a central photo.*

Monarchies may be a thing of the past, but in Bridgeport, Connecticut, they are alive and well in the form of the Barnum Festival's Royal Family. Coronated last April, the current king and Harvard hopeful, Daniel Schofield-Bodt has until this April to finish out his reign.

The Barnum Festival is a 55-year old tradition in the Greater Bridgeport Area initiated by the entertainer P.T. Barnum to instill community service and spirit. Each year, students in over 20 area schools compete for the titles of Barnum King, Queen, Prince and Princess. Together they work as good-will ambassadors for the festival.

Thirty-four students competed for the crowns in a demanding selection process. The first step was an interview in which community leaders held private sessions with each nominee.

"The first question they asked was 'tell us about yourself,'" Schofield-Bodt recalled. "I didn't know where to begin, but I took a deep breath and had a great interview."

Of course, there were some unexpected surprises.

"The best part of my interview came when the judges asked if it was true that I could juggle. I could tell they didn't really believe me, and they asked me to juggle the fruit that was on the table. So here I was in this boardroom, juggling fruit and doing tricks."

Candidates also took part in social events from a dance to a formal reception. Nominees mingled with judges and fellow candidates and were judged on social skills.

Winners were announced at the final event, a coronation ball, last April. Schofield-Bodt was crowned king and was joined by a queen, prince, and princess.

Together this group of students was inseparable, and attended over 20 events together over the summer of 2002 as the festival kicked into high gear.

"I have to say I was shocked at everything that went on," Schofield-Bodt said. "The whole thing was a much bigger production than I ever could have imagined. The whole city of Bridgeport was swept up in the spirit of the festival, and I got to go along on the magic ride."

The royal family concurred that the best perk was the motorcade.

"Everywhere we went we were escorted by cops," Schofield-Bodt explained. "After the fireworks at Seaside Park, the traffic was backed up for miles. The cops put their sirens on, took us on the wrong side of the road, and then led us onto the highway through the traffic jam back home. It was great."

The city of Bridgeport embraced these youths as the festival progressed.

"Of course, there were some people who would boo our motorcade, but most people whooped and cheered as we sat on top of convertibles waving. I remember at McDonalds on time our cashier got so excited that I was the Barnum Festival King and I got a free meal. This is easily the coolest thing I have ever done in high school." Thing became ever more interesting for Schofield-Bodt when he had surgery right in the middle of the festival.

"I had to have jaw surgery in the middle of June, and that was just a few weeks before the most important events. The doctors told me I wouldn't be able to get back into action because they had to put 14 screws and two metal plates in my mouth to hold everything together, but I knew I could make it back," he said.

After two weeks of a fluids-only diet, Schofield-Bodt was back in action with a brand new smile as the royal family attended the Jenny Lind Musical concert where two talented opera singers ended their Swedish and American tours with the Barnum Festival.

Two days later, Schofield-Bodt and company won best float in the Great Street Parade, the second largest parade in New England.

While the festival itself is over, Schofield-Bodt's reign will not close until next April. During the fall, Schofield-Bodt was juggling a full course load, making college decisions, and playing varsity soccer while participating in Barnum events such as the Wine Stomp and a Polo Match.

"I never want this carpet ride to end," said Schofield-Bodt. "It's been so awesome."

And to think the judges doubted that this young man could juggle. . . .

## ANALYSIS

Schofield-Bodt's essay appeals immediately to *Crimson* editors not only because it is written in the style of a newspaper article, but also because it makes a distinct and memorable first impression. Using third-person narrative techniques, Schofield-Bodt takes a unique approach in his essay describing his "reign" as Barnum king. The structure of the article is well done; Schofield-Bodt focuses the article on the Barnum Festival competition, and works in personal details around this central event. Taking us on a virtual trip over his junior spring and senior fall, Schofield-Bodt masterfully weaves together details and anecdotes about his juggling ability, his "royal motorcade," and his jaw surgery into the festival narrative. The choice of genre—a newspaper article—is a risky one, but Schofield-Bodt pulls it off well.

In carefully crafting a story with ups and downs, Schofield-Bodt avoids the risk of writing about oneself in the third-person: coming off as overly proud, or even arrogant. Instead, Schofield-Bodt uses the objective nature of a newspaper article to set a humble tone, writing in the style of a hometown paper. The juggling anecdote adds a nice touch, because it is an unusual talent and because Schofield-Bodt connects it with the last line of his essay.

The two things that Schofield-Bodt could have improved upon were proofreading and the formatting of the essay itself. Always proofread more than once yourself and enlist friends and family to proofread as well. As for the format, the essay was submitted as a scanned document with text wrapped around a central photo and a border down the sides, as well as some additional graphics. Watch out for making something too messy or complicated if you are thinking of doing something creative with the format. This particular essay is very strong, but its graphics take away a bit of its sophistication. If you are going to do something creative with design, stick with something simple and professional.

—Erica K. Jalli

# "To Freeze a Moment"

By Katya Rosenblatt, who attended a public high school in Belmont, Massachusetts, a suburb of Boston.

I rarely take pictures, and I no longer keep a regular diary. Garnering memories is a risky pastime.

Some years ago, writing in my journal used to be a customary activity. I would return from school and dedicate the expected half hour to diligently documenting the day's events, feelings, and impressions in my little blue leather-bound volume. I did not really need to vent my emotions by way of words, but I gained a certain satisfaction from seeing my experiences forever engraved on paper. After all, isn't sculpting memories a way of immortalizing the past?

When I was thirteen years old, I went hiking in Bryce Canyon, well-equipped with pens, journal, and camera. During the trip, I was obsessed with chronicling every occurrence, name and place I encountered. I felt proud to be spending my time productively, dutifully preserving for posterity a detailed account of my travels. On my last night there, I wandered out of my tent, diary in hand. The sky was illuminated by the glare of the moon, and the walls of the canyon looked menacing behind their veil of shadows. I instinctively reached for my pen . . .

At that point, I understood that nothing I wrote could ever parallel or replace the few seconds I allowed myself to experience the ineffable beauty of my surroundings. All I remembered of the previous few days were the dull characterizations I had set down in my journal. The sentences I had so tenderly molded sounded stale and bland. By stepping aside and constantly putting my adventures in perspective, I forgot to actually live them.

Now, I only write in my diary when I need to jot down a special thought or feeling. I still love to record ideas and quotations that strike me in books, or observations that are particularly meaningful. I take pictures, but not very often—only of objects I find irresistibly fascinating. I'm no longer infatuated with having something to remember when I grow old. I realize that life will simply pass me by if I stay behind the camera, too preoccupied with preserving the present so as to live it in the future.

I don't want to wake up one day and have nothing but a pile of pictures and notes. Maybe I won't have as many exact representations of people and places, maybe I'll forget certain facts, but at least the experiences will always remain inside me. I don't live to make memories— I just live, and the memories form themselves.

## ANALYSIS

Rosenblatt's essay relates a moment of epiphany that has defined her life-philosophy. Although works in this genre often fall into the trap of over-shooting their bounds, waxing eloquent to the point of strained profundity, this essay safely negotiates the line between pretension and maturity. In what is always a personal statement, Rosenblatt expresses the relevance of her reflections in terms of their effect upon her self. Her conclusion remains in the first person rather than employing the dreadful "we" that seems always to degenerate into pompous preaching or universal truths.

One of this essay's greatest strengths is its readability. Rosenblatt has appropriately sized this essay for her subject matter, enabling her to hold the reader's attention throughout the piece while avoiding rambling and repetition. The opening paragraph is particularly successful in drawing us in to the narrative that she is about to present. The bold phrase "garnering memories is a risky pastime" pulls the reader through the composition by prompting him or her to ask why, a question that is not answered until later in the piece.

A striking image or a particularly unique moment would strengthen this essay. After the fourth paragraph, when she reveals her conclusion, the essay becomes a little too predictable. By taking the safe path Rosenblatt avoids the risk of a negative reaction but, at the same time, does not leave the reader asking questions, inspired to find out more. Of course, every essay is a balance between the two, and Rosenblatt's essay—though not risk-taking—offers the reader an insight into who she is.

—Alicia M. DeSantis

# "Banana"

By Nathan W. Hill, who attended a small private school in Portland, Oregon.

I was hungry and the sun impaled me on its searing ray. I wore a wool coat, black with red cotton lining. It had served me well in the misty foothills of the Himalayas, where His Holiness, the Dalai Lama, gave his blessing. The coat had recently returned from a long absence. I wore it despite the heat.

The humid weather and the final wilting blossoms of late September conspired to fill my head with snot. The mighty hammer, Mjollnir, pounded his lament between my ears.

I walked down to The Barn, our cafeteria, but it wouldn't open again until three. Then, I remembered Clint, my junior year English teacher, and walked back to the Upper School. Clint always kept a few overripe bananas in the fruit bowl with the past due vocab tests. Laura, who shared the office, complained of the fetid smell of rotten fruit and that Clint made grunting noises as he worked hunched in his bow tie, over a mound of disheveled papers. On occasion, he stretched his arm towards Laura's desk and asked her, with a bruised banana dangling from his hand, "Would you like a banana, Laura?" With a crinkled nose, Laura always politely replied, "No, thank you, Clint," and watched in disgust as he wolfed it down.

The heavy wooden door to Clint's office stood propped open because of the heat. Inside, a small electric fan sat on top of the computer; it made an obnoxious noise between the sound of buzzing bees and chomping teeth. A tiny strip of paper darted before the spinning blades. Clint looked up from his work and asked with nasal condescension, "Can I help you, Nate?"

I responded phlegmatically, "May I have a banana?" the sweat dripping off the end of my nose.

With a mixture of pity and reproach, he raised his arm to point at the wooden bowl on top of the gray file cabinet. I lifted three vocab tests away.

I grabbed it, soft and brown. Its sweet aroma distracted me from the throbbing of my head. I held the banana in my right hand, and moved my left hand to its stem, ready to divest my prey.

A thin sticky liquid started seeping through my hand. Not expecting a banana to leak, I dropped it, and heard a low thud, followed by splattering.

The banana burst open; its mushy yellow guts flew. A dripping peel remained of my search for happiness.

## ANALYSIS

Hill has taken the basic narrative form in this essay and transformed it into something memorable. While Hill has alluded to the fact that he was in the Himalayas and that he was given a blessing by the Dalai Lama, he does not dwell on those events, however significant or unique. Rather, he chooses to concentrate on simple topics: hunger and a coveted banana.

The strength of Hill's essay rests with his descriptive language. The end of the essay particularly impacts the reader with vivid imagery. Few who read this essay will forget the image of an overripe banana exploding. Hill's phrasing is at times perfect: ". . . ready to divest my prey," is one such example of convincing, powerful language. Hill has conveyed the exact magnitude of his hunger and desire for that banana with this phrase.

A few areas could be strengthened, however. Hill is somewhat meandering in his opening, touching on topics like the Dalai Lama and the Himalayas, which, though interesting, are not significant to the main thrust of the narrative. Also, Hill's use of dialogue and the description of Clint and Laura are a little awkward. He might have done better to have simply expanded upon the latter paragraphs of his essay, focusing more on the banana and his hunger and omitting this dialogue and the description of Clint. Despite these small complications, Hill has done the trick and produced an essay that demands attention and respect.

—Adam S. Cohen

# "A Night Unforgotten"

By Frederick Antwi, who attended Ghana International School in Ghana, West Africa.

An hour before the commencement of the personality contest, I deposited my bag carefully in a corner of the changing room. From my vantage point, I could see the muscular seniors comparing their lovely three-piece suits and musing about which one of them would win the title. A bony, stuttering junior with no suit and no new shoes, I swallowed hard and resolved to give the pageant my best shot. Since the first round of the program was a parade in traditional wear, I nervously pulled out my kente, draped the beautifully woven red and yellow fabric around my thin frame, pinned on my "contestant number five" badge and hurried to take my place in line.

Wishing hopelessly that my mother was among the spectators and not working in some hospital in a foreign country, I stepped out onto the polished wooden stage. Immediately, one thousand two hundred curious eyes bore into me. My cheeks twitched violently, my throat constricted and my knees turned to jelly. I fought for control. Bending my arms slightly at the elbows, I strutted across the stage in the usual fashion of an Asante monarch and mercifully made it back to the changing room without mishap. The crowd erupted into a frenzied cheer. As I returned for the "casual wear" round, something magical happened.

It was a singular emotion that no words can describe. It began as an aching, beautiful tenderness in the pit of my stomach, gradually bubbling into my chest, filling me with warmth and radiance, melting away all the tension. Slowly, it effervesced into my mouth, onto my tongue and into words. As I spoke to the crowd of my pastimes and passions, words of such silky texture poured out from my soul with unparalleled candor and cadence. The voice that issued from my lips was

at once richer, deeper, stronger than I had ever produced. It was as
though an inner self, a core essence, had broken free and taken control. Severed from reality, I floated through the remainder of that remarkable evening.

One hour later, the baritone of the presenter rang out into the cool
night air. "Mr. GIS Personality 1993, selected on the basis of confidence, charisma, cultural reflection, style, eloquence, wit and original-
ity, is Contestant number . . ."

"Five! One! Five! Five!" roared the electrified crowd.

My heart pounded furiously. My breathing reduced to shallow
gasps.

"Contestant number five!" exploded the presenter in confirmation.

For a few sacred moments, time stopped. My ears screamed, and my
lower jaw, defying the grip of my facial muscles, dropped like a draw-
bridge. Then I rushed forward, bear-hugged the presenter and embraced everyone else I could lay my hands on! Amidst the tumult, the
Manager of KLM Airlines mounted the stage, presenting me with a
meter-long Accra-Amsterdam-London return ticket. As I stood bran-
dishing my sky-blue cardboard ticket, posing shamelessly for the cameras and grinning sheepishly at the throng, a pang of regret shot
through me. If only my mother could have been in that crowd to witness and indeed be a part of this most poignant of all memories.

## ANALYSIS

"The unusual experience" is a staple of college entrance essays, but in this
case the experience is truly unusual—a personality contest for men? It's
also interesting to see Antwi's transformation from shy to superstar. Antwi
concentrates on a fixed event in time and uses it to show the spectrum of
his personality—shy, confident, excited, lonely—in an amusing and entertaining way.

It's no wonder Antwi won the contest. He's a great storyteller. He has an acute sense of detail—"one thousand two hundred curious eyes," "the fashion of an Asante monarch"—and is good at heightening drama. The essay is also upbeat and fun to read.

It would have been nice to know what Antwi said in the third paragraph instead of simply reading about the "unparalleled candor and cadence" with which he spoke. Also, Antwi does not explain the what, where, or why of the contest, which are all important to know. Overall, however, his personality shines through as stellar.

—Caille M. Millner

# "A Lesson About Life"

By Aaron Miller, who attended a large public school in Aptos, California.

Finally the day had arrived. I was on my way to Aspen, Colorado. I had heard wonderful stories about the Aspen Music School from friends who had attended in previous years, and I was certain that this summer would be an unbelievable learning experience. I was especially excited to be studying with Mr. Herbert Stessin, an esteemed professor from the Juilliard School.

After just a few lessons with Mr. Stessin, I knew that I would not be disappointed. Mr. Stessin is so incredibly sharp that no detail gets by him. He notices every turn of each musical phrase, catches wrong notes in complex chords, and interjects his wry sense of humor into every lesson. As I was preparing Beethoven's Sonata, Op. 31, No. 3, for a master class, he warned me at the end of a lesson, "Don't play this too well, Aaron, or I'll have nothing to say!"

The master class went quite well considering that it was my first performance of the sonata. A few days later, as I walked across the bridge over the creek which winds through the music school campus, I saw Mr. Stessin's wife, Nancy, who was also on the Aspen faculty. I waved to her, and as I walked past she said something to me which I didn't catch over the roar of the rushing water. I stopped for a moment as she repeated, "That was a very nice Beethoven you played the other day." We had a brief conversation, and I was touched by her thoughtful comment.

On July 15 I had my last lesson with Mr. Stessin, and walked with him to the dining hall. As I was sitting down with my friends to have lunch, someone whispered to me, "Mrs. Stessin passed out!" We naturally assumed that she had fainted from the altitude or the heat. However, we soon realized that the situation was more serious, as an ambulance was called to take her to the nearby hospital.

Nothing could have prepared me for the news that two distraught friends brought late that night to my roommate and me. Mrs. Stessin had never regained consciousness and had died of a ruptured aneurysm. That night, my roommate and I could not sleep; we talked about our memories of Mrs. Stessin for hours on end. In the morning, Dean Laster called us together to officially announce the sad news.

Numb with disbelief that this vibrant and dedicated woman was gone, we wondered how Mr. Stessin could possibly cope with this terrible tragedy. Surely he would be heading back to New York as soon as arrangements could be made.

I couldn't have been more wrong. Only days later, Mr. Stessin was back in his studio, teaching!

Initially shocked by Mr. Stessin's decision to stay, I soon began to understand his thinking. He and his wife had been teaching at Aspen for many years and had built a strong sense of community with the faculty and students. Furthermore, I realized that he found comfort through his love of music and his commitment to his students. Leaving Aspen would have meant leaving behind his fondest memories of Nancy.

After studying a Mozart piano concerto with Mr. Stessin all summer, I was fortunate to win the Nakamichi Piano Concerto competition, but even more fortunate to have the opportunity to dedicate my performance to the memory of Mrs. Stessin. At the end of the concert, my last evening in Aspen, I was greeted by friends and faculty members backstage. When I saw Mr. Stessin approaching me, he was beaming. "That was a wonderful performance!" he said, and gave me a hug. He continued, "And thank you for the dedication. I'll miss you." We hugged again.

Last summer did indeed turn out to be an unbelievable learning experience. Although Mr. Stessin taught me a great deal about music and the piano, in the end his greatest lesson was about life.

## ANALYSIS

Miller builds a strong essay around two big stories: a phenomenal accomplishment and a moving death.

He has a good ear for coupling dialogue and narration, and projects himself with attractive modesty. Miller offers the reader a chance to appreciate an especially wide range of qualities: empathy, virtuosity, wisdom, and generosity, although he misses a good opportunity to describe how he feels about the music he performs, and his conclusion is somewhat trite.

Miller limits his essay to a scope that makes sense. Relating a personal tragedy can be key to allowing the reader to appreciate one's maturity, but one must have a gentle touch and healthy emotional distance.

—Matthew A. Carter

# "Running Thoughts"

By Nikhil Kacker, who attended a small suburban public high school in
Northbrook, Illinois.

I closed my eyes and slowly took a deep breath. The gun rang loudly
in my ears as the runners sprinted out of the start, pushing and
shoving for the lead. I ran out with a fast, long stride, trying to keep my
breathing even, while counting my strides in my head. I threw elbows
to my left and right as we jostled for position. As the lead group turned
the first corner, I lost count when my leg hit a cone on the course. Veer-
ing towards the outside, I cut someone off behind me and heard a yell
of protest. Suddenly, I was flying towards the ground.

My hands scraped the gravel on my way down, stinging with pain.
Someone had tripped me! Quickly, I pushed myself up from the dirt
and sprinted back to the lead, heart pounding frantically in my chest.
That was a stupid move; I almost cost the race for the whole team. I
suddenly felt weak; instead of running, I was dragging my body.

As I plodded on, thoughts of marching band practice later in the
day brought our show abruptly into my head. I began running to the
beat of "Robin Hood." I found strength and energy flow into my body.
My limbs suddenly seemed lighter and more flexible, ready to be
pushed even further.

"Nikhil, let's keep moving. Keep the pace up!" shouted my coach
from the mile mark. I started pumping my arms harder, propelling myself faster. Widening the gap between the other runners and myself, I
fell into a rhythm. Everything seems to be in harmony, just like Lao-
Tzu believed. I suddenly thought of the history paper I had to write on
Taoism this weekend. It was going to take so long that I doubted I
would be able to go out with friends tonight. My shoulders began to
tighten and I felt my lungs turn to lead.

Thump, thump. I glanced behind and saw a runner within twenty feet of me. My heart skipped a beat while I raced ahead and increased my lead. Reaching the gravel pavement, my spiked shoes created a pulsating crackle on the hard rocks. The grating roar of pebbles which the waves suck back and fling at their return. Sitting on the pebble beach in Nice with friends, laughing and joking. The warm sun enveloped me. A smile spread across my face.

The roar of the crowd near the finish sent renewed energy into my exhausted legs. Turning the last corner, my mind went blank; all I felt was a force pushing me towards the end, causing me to sprint faster and faster. Crossing the line, I collapsed in the grass, heaving and panting. I had won, I had won. That's all that went through my mind. As I struggled to catch my breath, I reminded myself, as after every race: "Each race is a drama, a challenge. Each race stretches me one way and another and each race tells me more about myself and others."

## ANALYSIS

This essay effectively combines the details of a specific event in the author's high school career as well as her general interests and experiences. The reader learns that the writer not only enjoys competitive track but that she likes marching band, studying history, and traveling. We learn that the writer is multidimensional and get a glimpse of how she balances all these interests. Small details, such as hearing the sounds of "Robin Hood," are integrated so that the essay is not simply a list of her extracurricular activities, but actually a look inside the mind of the writer captured in those few minutes of the race.

The overall tone of the essay is effective in conveying the excitement of the race, but the writer is also careful to break the monotone of describing that one event with the constant shift back to her mental thoughts on the other aspects of her life. This is also reflected in the variation of sentence structure, which helps keep the reader's attention.

Although we do learn a lot about the writer's interests in this essay, discussing more about why she enjoys them is a possible area of improvement. In addition, while the concluding quote ties in the story nicely, citing a quote at the end of an essay often results in the loss of the personal voice of the writer and should be considered carefully.

—Nancy Poon

# "Playing the Giramel's Behind"

By Eliot I. Hodges, who attended a small private high school in
Washington, D.C.

In the Washington Opera's production of Mozart's "The Magic
Flute," Tamino, the Singsmiel's protagonist, charms fantastic, hy-
brid animals such as the Pantelot, the Ostremu, and the Chimpaboon
into following him by playing a mellifluous melody on his magical
flute. If you have had the opportunity to enjoy this opera at the
Kennedy Center, then you must have also seen a nine-foot tall concoc-
tion of a giraffe and a camel known as a Giramel waddling among its
fellow fauna. I played its posterior.

As the Giramel's behind, not much of me was to be seen, since my
legs, which were dressed in Pepto-Bismol–colored tights, and my feet,
masqueraded as gigantic, cartoon-like hooves, were my only visible
parts—the rest was neatly tucked into the vast wire-and-foam interior
of the pink behemoth. As sprightly as the Giramel might have appeared on stage, it demanded considerable doing on my part to help
animate the animal, be it through a shuffle of hoof, a shake of hip, or a
swirl of tail. I needed a lot of practice.

Two months to be exact, but when using a "practice/real-time con-
version scale," this translates into five minutes of real stage time per
performance. There were eleven performances.

Despite being a supernumerary, the pawn of the opera hierarchy, I
had a passion for bringing the Giramel's derrière to life. This was
partly due to my recall of Sherlock Holmes' words: "It has long been an
axiom of mine that the little things are infinitely the most important."
This, of course, is an obvious overstatement of my position as the invisible puppeteer of the Giramel's nether set of cheeks, but it helped
explain a sentiment I have about the arts: be it a mere street-crosser in
a spaghetti Western or a triangle's chime in a symphony, everything is

of inherent value to the finished product—provided, of course, that it is done well.

Thus, I saw my Giramel career as being much like one of the specks in Jackson Pollack's "No. 9"—almost undiscernible when standing alone, but of value when seen as a part of the whole.

## ANALYSIS

This essay, an example of a unique personal experience, mixes humor and culture to form a lethal one-two punch. Appearing on the Kennedy Center stage is something of which to be proud, even if it is as the rump of an imaginary animal. Hodges does well to show who he is—he has a sense of humor, he is a good writer and he is obviously a talented performer. (Do you realize how hard it would be to shake *that* booty?)

It is not uncommon for a college applicant to write about his role as the lead in a high school, community, or even professional performance and how much he learned from it. Hodges has set himself apart from these people in the first paragraph by admitting to something most would want to forget about. True, he does go on to tell how valuable an experience it was, but *anyone* would learn from that experience—at the very least a lesson in humility. Humility is probably the best character trait to write about. It lets you talk about yourself without being too cocky.

Hodges's essay is not perfect, however. Despite his writing talent, his sentences tend to be long and brimming with clauses. The admissions officer who reads the essay will likely have been reading essays all day. While Hodges has set himself apart, long sentences can turn the reader off fast. You are not going to prove that you are the next Dickens in fewer than five hundred words. On the flip side, if you tend too much toward Hemingway, you might want to beef up your writing with some color. Description is good, but not to the point where it slows down the pace of the essay.

—William P. Bohlen

# "Truly Alive"

By James Collins, who attended a medium-sized public school in Dix Hills, New York.

A jump turn and through Gate B I entered a new world. It was a world of exhilaration; a world of beauty, of love, of hope and of serenity. "Watch out for that boulder!" "Tree on your left!" "Follow that line!" were such simple survival commands we uttered as explorers of this terra incognita. Blood rushed, spirits flew, and minds soared. The world we once knew was a distant memory, a long-forgotten thing of the past. The mere three and a half hours spent in our paradise fills me with a lifetime of stirring memories.

It was Killebrew Canyon on the Nevada side of Lake Tahoe's Heavenly Mountain. Of the two canyons, Killebrew is certainly the road less traveled. Warning signs are posted everywhere alerting skiers and boarders to the treacherous trek back to the Mott Canyon lift (the only way home). Killebrew is a desolate and hidden area. Protected by its entrance gates and warning signs and lying well off the beaten path, it is a well-kept secret. One place, one world, I never would have found had I not met two people I will never forget.

Riding up the Dipper Express, I couldn't help but ask my lift-mates if they had skied the Dipperknob Trees. The area looked interesting on the map and caught my eye. They hadn't been there. I was a bit disappointed, but I found easy conversation about the amazing if not perfect ski conditions. It had snowed over a foot the night before leaving a powdery white blanket across the land. I soon asked the two people, presumably a married couple, where they had been on the mountain. They spoke as if they had seen something unearthly. Their words, inviting to a skier's soul, left me no other choice than to follow them to Killebrew.

We skied across the mountain and glided into the woods where Gate B emerged into view. They warned me that the canyon would eat anything less than an expert skier. With a gulp, I accepted their challenge and quickly asked them about the long trek mentioned on the warning sign. They chuckled a bit, and I dared not ask any further questions. We then crossed into paradise. I gasped at the beauty. The pristine blue sky, the majestic trees, the foreboding cliffs, the perfectly white surface. It was the first time I had ever seen something of such ineffable beauty. The colors and dancing light were like transcendent chords of a musical masterpiece that had taken on visible form—euphoric tones transformed into snowdrifts, icicles, and evergreens. Everything collapsed into the simplicity that surrounded me. And suddenly they were skiing; I had to follow.

They flowed down the mountain with liquid precision in perfect harmony. We dodged trees, jumped cliffs, and navigated waist-high powder. It was true adventure, as we fought and found our way down. Jump turns, knee bends, and pole plants kept us from being consumed by the mountain. And as we hit the bottom I too chuckled. There was no trek. It was a short and scenic trail right to the lift. Certainly, it is no mistake that Killebrew is kept a secret.

As the day warmed up, conversation flowed, and ski masks were removed. I found myself shocked that I had been skiing with a retired couple in their sixties. My respect for their skiing abilities slowly grew into admiration for who they were. They were kind and peaceful, wise and without pretense. As the last run of the day approached I decided to go off on my own and explore a few parts of Killebrew that we hadn't seen. I reached the bottom rather quickly and waited for my newfound friends. Five minutes passed and I wished that I was still skiing. But five minutes soon turned into half an hour, and I began to worry. Thoughts rushed through my head. I feared the mountain had claimed the two people I thought would live forever. But, as I was on my way to the Ski Patrol, I heard a noise in the woods. It was them!

I had to hold myself back from running up and hugging them. They had no clue how long they had been gone. They simply told me they took their time and thanked me for waiting for them. The ski day was over. I went one way, they the other. I never saw them again. Their memory fulfills my definitions of love, hope, beauty, and serenity. And now, whenever I see a perfect blue sky or perhaps feel a cool breeze, I am reminded of my friends and of that day when I was truly alive.

## ANALYSIS

In his essay, Collins recalls his ski trip to Killebrew Canyon—an extremely memorable experience for him. What is striking about this piece is its descriptiveness. Through Collins's thorough painting of the surrounding settings, one realizes the breathtaking beauty of his environment. The essay carries the reader fluidly through its eloquent narrative; one is almost able to see the landscape flash by through Collins's eyes.

However, weighing in at almost eight hundred words, the essay is a little long. Also, the essay's focus remains rather ambiguous. Was the Killebrew episode an example of how Collins's willingness to accept challenges opened up a new "paradise" for him? Or was the essay about the bonds of friendship forged during the trip? And, what was the purpose of the tension created when Collins's friends failed to show up on time? These are some of the critical questions which remain unanswered. This dichotomous approach to the essay—alternatively describing the scenery or the couple—creates uncertainty about what the essay is ultimately trying to say.

And one cannot help but sense that the generalizations the essay attempts to make are too broad. Collins says at the end of the essay that his brief encounter with the couple "fulfills [his] definitions of love, hope, beauty, and serenity." Yet, if the crux of the essay is how the couple gave him a new standard for love, hope, and beauty, then where is the basis for comparison? Collins's prose crackles with life as he reminds us that what matters most is the feeling of being "truly alive."

—Risheng Xu

# "Checkmate"

By Robert M. Stolper, who attended a public high school in New City,
New York.

S word in hand, the black knight leapt forward and in one mighty
swing fell the king's loyal guard. The king backed away, a feeling
of helplessness washing over him. Suddenly, one of the knight's hench-
men, spiked mace in hand, appeared behind the king, trapping the
ruler. Nowhere to go. Nothing to do. The king knew it was over.

I pushed the chess piece over in disgust. Another game, another
loss. This was becoming monotonous. I played chess with my grandfather maybe once a month. And almost every time I lost. He knew the
moves and maneuvers, the counters and the attacks. But most of all, he
knew me. "Good game, Robby," my grandfather said. He stood, fixed
his silk shirt and Brooks Brothers tie, and winked. "You had a couple
of good moves, but you've got to keep thinking." He gave me a hug.
"Good game."

Whenever we're together, my grandfather and I always seem to end
up playing chess. We usually play late into the night, listening to classical music and discussing world events. I can remember one particular night, when we played until three-thirty in the morning.

It was like any other game. Each move took my grandfather three or
four minutes. He carefully planned each action, contemplated every
possible countermaneuver, and then double checked to see if he forgot
any conceivable move. That is why he's so difficult to beat. And why
he's so difficult to play. He thinks like he plays: careful, deliberate,
and precise. It's taken me a while to understand him. In fact, it's taken
me a while to understand myself. Not everything can be seen as easily
as in chess. Not all moves are as predictable; not all decisions are as
defined. As I look back on the games I've played with my grandfather,
I wonder if he knows how much he's really taught me. That patience is

learned; that concentration is developed; that persistence pays off in the end. I wonder if I should tell him.

We sat down for yet another game of chess. At first, the battle went poorly for me. My forces were in retreat, and I had to sacrifice piece after piece to protect my king. Down went my bishop, down went my rook, down went my queen. But I slowed the pace of the game, and changed retreat to advance. I contemplated each move, and after a while I had his king surrounded. Then, in a surprise maneuver, his king took my knight. "Nice move, Grandpa," I said as I slid my rook forward. "Checkmate."

He taught me more than he knew. "Good game, Robby. Good game."

## ANALYSIS

This essay demonstrates how one specific event or moment in a person's daily life can be used to reflect the character and inner workings of the author. This type of essay is frequently used and, if done properly, can show what is really important to the applicant. Whether it be playing an instrument in the school orchestra, playing tennis on your varsity team, or playing chess with your grandfather, an essay describing the feelings surrounding the action is what counts. An essay in this genre gives the author a chance to give a more personal and emotional feeling to the admissions application.

The strength in this essay is its simplicity. Stolper creatively introduces the relationship between himself and his grandfather through a common interest—chess. We can see that Stolper enjoys his time with his grandfather and the challenge to improve his own game. The introduction is especially intriguing. We don't initially know what to expect or what the essay is about. The detailed illustration of the king's futile situation is much more exciting than if Stolper had simply told us he was playing chess. As the essay progresses, the relationship further unfolds. The use of dialogue allows the reader to envision the two characters playing the game. By the end, we want and expect Stolper to win. This essay is truly enjoyable to read. It is the simplicity of the characters as well as the story that make it work.

One area for improvement might be the casual mention of personal improvement near the end of the essay. In the fourth paragraph, Stolper writes, "It's taken me a while to understand myself." Unfortunately, there is no development of this point. How has he come to understand himself and what has he learned? Although an explanation might distract the reader from the focus of the essay, the reader is more concerned with the development of the grandson.

—Daniel A. Shapiro

# INFLUENCES

# "Dandelion Dreams"

By Emmeline Chuang, who attended a large public high school in New York City.

My big sister once told me that if I shut my eyes and blew on a dandelion puff, all of my wishes would come true. I used to believe her and would wake up early in the morning to go dandelion hunting. How my parents must have laughed to see me scrambling out in the backyard, plucking little gray weeds, and blowing out the seeds until my cheeks hurt.

I made the most outrageous wishes. I wished to own a monkey, a parrot, and a unicorn; I wished to grow up and be just like She-Ra, Princess of Power. And, of course, I wished for a thousand more wishes so I would never run out.

I always believed my wishes would come true. When they didn't, I ran to my sister and demanded an explanation. She laughed and said I just hadn't done it right.

"It only works if you do it a certain way," she told me with a little smile. I watched her with wide, admiring eyes and thought she must be right. She was ten years older than me and knew the ways of the world; nothing she said could be wrong. I went back and tried again.

Time passed, and I grew older. My "perfect" sister left home—not telling my parents where she had gone. Shocked by her apparent fall from grace, I spent most of my time staring out the window. I wondered where she had gone and why she hadn't told us where she was going. Occasionally, I wandered outside to pluck a few dandelions and wish for my sister's return. Each time, I hoped desperately that I had done it the right way and that the wish would come true.

But it never happened.

After a while, I gave up—not only on my sister—but on the dandelions as well. Shock had changed to anger and then to rejection of my sister and everything she had told me. The old dreamer within me vanished and was replaced by a harsh teenage cynic who told me over and over that I should have known better than to believe in free wishes. It chided me for my past belief in unicorns and laughed at the thought of my growing up to be a five foot eleven, sleek She-Ra. It told me to stop being silly and sentimental and to realize the facts of life, to accept what I was and what my sister was, and live with it.

For a while I tried. I abandoned my old dreams, my old ideas, and threw myself entirely into school and the whole dreary rat race of scrabbling for grades and popularity. After a time, I even began to come out ahead and could start each day with an indifferent shrug instead of a defeated whimper. Yet none of it made me happy. For some reason, I kept on thinking about dandelions and my sister.

I tried to forget about both, but the edge of my anger and disillusionment wore away and the essence of my old self started to seep through again. Despite the best efforts of the cynic in me, I continually found myself staring out at those dandelions—and making wishes.

It wasn't the same as before, of course. Most of my old dreams and ideals had vanished forever. Certainly, I could never wish for a unicorn as a pet and actually mean it now. No, my dreams were different now, less based on fantasy and more on reality.

Dreams of becoming a princess in a castle or a magical sorceress had changed into hopes of someday living in the woods and writing novels like J. D. Salinger, or playing Tchaikovsky's Concerto in A to orchestral accompaniment. These were the dreams that floated through my mind now. They were tempered by a caution that hadn't been there before, but they were there. For the first time since my sister's departure, I was acknowledging their presence.

I had to, for it was these dreams that diluted the pure meaninglessness of my daily struggles in school and made me happy. It was these dreams and the hope of someday fulfilling them that ultimately saved me from falling into the clutches of the dreaded beast of apathy that lurked alongside the trails of the rat race. Without them, I think I would have given up and stumbled off the tracks long ago.

It took a long time for me to accept this truth and to admit that my cynical self was wrong in denying me my dreams, just as my youthful self had been wrong in living entirely within them. In order to succeed and survive, I needed to find a balance between the two.

My sister was right; I hadn't been going after my dreams the right way. Now I know better. This time around, when I go into the garden and pick my dandelion puff, my wishes will come true.

## ANALYSIS

This essay works by portraying the immense effect of a single experience upon the life of the author. The writer's strength lies not in her language or her rhetoric, but in the narrative that she tells. It is the experience itself that actually makes this essay successful. The story is indeed a compelling one and the reader leaves the page with a desire to know more about Chuang.

The beginning of the essay works especially well in slowly captivating the reader. The opening is strong. Though it could be taken as artificial, the vivid image of the girl in the dandelions nevertheless grabs our attention. The steady progression of the narrative climaxes in the sixth paragraph, as the pointedly bold statement "but it never happened" takes the reader by surprise. At this moment, the reader is fully engaged in Chuang's narrative.

In fact, the reader is so drawn in by Chuang's story that the essay's rambling in the second half is frustrating. Perhaps this problem could have been alleviated had the author spent more time elaborating upon a specific moment in her struggle with this experience.

In the end, the sincerity at the heart of the narrative is very redeeming. The very tone of the narrative expresses a great deal about the author. Ultimately, Chuang is not merely a name at the top of the page, but a real person, with a real experience that an admissions officer can remember.

—Alicia M. DeSantis

# "*Lyubov* and *Viktoria*"

By Viktoria Slavina, who attended a large public magnet school in New York City.

Lyubov means "love" in Russian. My mother, Lyubov, truly loved life. She always found joy in simple things—smelling the sweet scent of jasmine from a nearby bush, sipping Earl Grey with a friend, spending hours in front of one painting at a museum, or playing a perfect sonata on the piano.

My mother was diagnosed with ovarian cancer in 1995. Even though she had countless chemotherapy sessions and several operations, she never complained. Despite her deteriorating health, my mother lived an active life and took pleasure in all aspects of it. Lyubov was a musician and her passion for music endured. She continued her studies and received a teacher's license. She worked as a substitute teacher at my elementary school, gave piano lessons, attended Parent Association meetings, played piano for my fourth grade production of *The King and I,* and watched my brother and me graduate from our respective schools. She did all this with a wig covering her head and while visiting Memorial Sloan Kettering Hospital weekly for treatment.

My mother held tenaciously to the life she so loved. Bravely and without hesitation, she chose to undergo difficult treatments and to take strong medications. My mother's perseverance allowed her to live with cancer for three years. When my family brought her to the hospital for the last time she still tried to be strong and even joked with the doctor.

Victoria means "victory" in Latin. My name, Viktoria, represents Lyubov's battle to have a child; she had several miscarriages prior to my conception. My mother endowed me not only with this name, but also with an unrelenting spirit.

I think of my mother daily and try to be as strong as she was. While I am not a talented musician, I am a passionate athlete. From a young age, I have enjoyed dance and gymnastics because they allow me to use my body as an instrument of expression, strength and control. My love for athletics, however, was threatened when I dislocated my ankle several years ago and had to undergo surgery. It would have been easy to just give up sports but, thinking of my mother, I took the more difficult path and persevered. Many hours of physical therapy later, my ankle healed and I was even able to become a competitive diver. From my mother I learned that the passions in life are worth fighting for.

My mother also bestowed me with intellectual curiosity and a love for learning. I take this with me every day; I read past the assigned chapters in schoolbooks, I ask my teachers questions and take my academic interests beyond the classroom. My mother taught me that the world must be understood in order to be appreciated.

Victory is the daughter of love. Without passion and dedication, success is unattainable. As Lyubov's daughter, I have vowed to continue her legacy. I try to handle adversity with courage and urgency and to take nothing for granted. And I always remember to walk through life enjoying the sweet scent of jasmine, for Lyubov and for Viktoria.

## ANALYSIS

In this well-crafted essay, Slavina takes a common theme for college essays—the trials of an illness in a family—and crafts a piece that is elegant, readable, and original. Rather than focus on the obvious, that her mother's illness and death played a major role in her formation into a young adult, Slavina begins the piece with the meaning of her mother's name and how it is connected to her own; she tells us of her mother's bravery and then reflects on her own accomplishments. In doing so, she demonstrates her compassion, openness, and a nuanced sense of family history.

What really makes Slavina's essay extraordinary, though, is her fluid prose. Slavina does not use hackneyed words or make grandiose statements; she keeps it simple, and the result is a clear, moving piece that seems natural, not forced. An essay that grapples with the weighty subject of a death in the family could tend toward the maudlin, but Slavina demonstrates her maturity and confidence in an understated style. Her choice not to mention cancer until the second paragraph lends the subject added force, and we realize that the essay will not be about cancer, but about her mother's bravery and love. Slavina's essay is an excellent example of the "show, don't tell" strategy; she lets her vivid descriptions and imagery express their own power without being heavy-handed.

One thing Slavina leaves out—perhaps intentionally—is any information about the circumstances of her mother's death or any time frame. We are told that she lived three years after the diagnosis, and that she perservered through treatments while being an attentive mother, but little else. While the absence of such details serves to highlight her mother's unflinching devotion, Slavina might have fleshed out more about her personal relationship with her mother and the direct effect Lyubov's illness had on her at the time. Since her essay is so tightly wrought, Slavina could have afforded more words for this kind of detail. At the same time, she could have tightened up, or eliminated, discussion of her injury in sports, which seems insignificant in comparison to her mother's illness. Slavina also takes a great risk in focusing so heavily on her mother in so short an essay. Nonetheless, Slavina succeeds in conveying her message, loud and clear, by means of the essay's tight structure and simple language.

—Rebecca D. O'Brien

# "A Great Influence"

By Michelangelo V. D'Agostino, who attended a small Catholic school in Chicago, Illinois.

Albert Einstein must have been a truly quirky individual. Though a patent officer by day, he worked into the wee hours of the morning on his revolutionary theories. I can just see him with his mass of white hair splayed out on his desk catching up on some long-overdue sleep. Of all the science teachers that I have ever had, only one has been comparable to Albert Einstein; only one has been able to truly appreciate physics like Einstein and been able to instill this deep appreciation in others.

Mr. Michael Peterson walked into the classroom for the first day of AP Physics flouting the standard notions of a teacher at St. Ignatius. He wore khaki shorts, an open-necked golf shirt, and deck shoes with no socks. The most striking features of his appearance were the two dark blue semi-circles underneath his eyes. He appeared to be somewhere between a raccoon and a test subject for a psychological experiment on sleep deprivation. He was always to be found holding a mug of caffeinated beverage, whether it be Pepsi, Jolt, or Mountain Dew. He went on to inform us that he did not sleep much (as if we couldn't already tell), between teaching and working on his own theories. Like Einstein, he loved what he was doing, and he spent as much time as possible pursuing his goals.

His method of teaching was also unlike any I had previously experienced. He emphasized pragmatism and creativity through hands-on projects and creative writing assignments. One of the major projects that we pursued was the building of a go-cart. For three weeks we hammered and greased our way into a better understanding of what we were studying. One of the major problems we encountered was with the brake system: we just couldn't figure out how to make it work. With a wry smile on his face, Mr. Peterson said, "I would advise that you figure it out. Brakes are a pretty important part of a car." He taught us that the answer will not always be in a book. There will not always be a teacher to swoop down like a guardian angel with all the answers. We successfully worked out the problem ourselves, and our brakes were able to stop on a dime. Okay, maybe a quarter. Einstein once said that knowledge is nothing without imagination. Mr. Peterson truly comprehended this ideal and stood behind it.

Obviously his methods worked. People were interested in science, and grades reflected it. We all looked forward to coming to class every day. The administration did not appreciate his efforts though. He was told that he must either teach from the text in a more orthodox manner, or he must leave. He said that it would be unfair to sell his students down the river. Consequently, he lost his job.

Towards the end of the year, Mr. Peterson faced his uncertain future with composure. He said that for all he knew he might be flipping greasy hamburgers this time next year, but he didn't mind. If Albert Einstein was a patent officer, why couldn't a fast-food worker revolutionize science? Someday Mr. Michael Peterson could be receiving the Nobel Prize for physics. And you know what? I wouldn't be the least bit surprised. He taught me to love science, to value creativity, and to be true to my ideals. In this way he has forever influenced my life.

## ANALYSIS

The essay highlights aspects of the author's personality via an examination of how that personality has been affected by another individual, in this case, an unorthodox schoolteacher. The essay proceeds by describing this teacher, and his interaction with the author, concluding with a description of how that interaction has imparted upon the author a series of important lessons in both science and in life.

What makes the essay work is its strong sense of organization. The reader is taken smoothly from the enticing introduction, through the description of the author's teacher, to the eventual conclusion of the teacher being fired and the author's reflection on the teacher's influence. The essay's use of analogies and similarities is also effective. The description of the teacher's independent work in physics strengthens the reader's appreciation for the lessons of independent thought and problem-solving that seem to be imparted upon the author through his classroom experiences. The analogy between the author's teacher and famous theoretical physicist Albert Einstein also showcases the author's appreciation for another one of life's ironic lessons—that sometimes the most brilliant minds and teachers are also the most unorthodox and misunderstood ones.

The essay could be improved, however, by giving us a better background on the author's views and ideals prior to his interaction with the physics teacher. Although the reader is given a clear view of what lessons the author has learned via this interaction, it is not clear as to how much of a transformation has truly occurred in the author's character. By describing the author's character prior to his experiences with the teacher, the essay could serve to better position these experiences within the course of the author's development.

—Elliot Shmukler

# "Michael and Me"

By Brian R. McElroy

Michael is my best friend. I would trust him with my life. We have known each other and attended the same schools since first grade. We played on Little League and basketball teams together, and we lifted weights at his house every day after school. Our relationship was the epitome of male bonding.

Michael has significantly influenced the person I have become. In school he strives for excellence and achieves it. He has a unique ability to relate to people. He is committed, driven and self-confident. Emotionally, he is the strongest person I know. These are qualities that I also see in myself. Just as I appreciate Michael's qualities, he appreciates mine; when I asked Michael for three words to describe me, his answers were "loyal, driven and optimistic." I am committed to giving respect to those who are entitled to it, such as my parents, teachers and coaches. My friends and teammates are extremely important to me. My drive, self-confidence and willingness to chance failure have allowed me to take on challenges others might not consider. These challenges define my life by constantly providing inspiration. I try to live my life according to a Japanese proverb: "Fall seven times, stand up eight." Lastly, I have always been an optimist, and I love to laugh. My friends and family marvel at my jovial nature. Many times my family had considered placing me on a respirator after hearing me erupt in laughter at a Dave Barry book or an episode of *The Simpsons*.

Last year, Michael told me he was gay. I was dumbfounded. Looking back, I realized that I had failed to notice emerging signs of his sexuality. I wondered how I, his best friend, could have failed to see them. Friends had approached me and asked if Michael was gay. My answer was always, "Of course not!" Then I realized why his revelation came as a shock. My closest friends are those that I not only admire but emulate. Michael has played a major part in shaping my personality. In fact, our friends often comment that we "share a brain." I never considered that he might be gay because I knew I was not.

I soon found that I had no problem with Michael's sexuality. I realized that he had helped me to reject prejudices and accept people for who they are. "Coming out of the closet" was an ordeal for Michael, and it took every ounce of his emotional strength to deal with it. While he always told himself that I knew him better than anyone else and that he could tell me anything, he hid himself from me. Now that I know, our relationship has become stronger, and we know that nothing will ever come between us.

His courage inspired me to participate in the September 1997 Boston–New York AIDS Ride 3. I did not even have a bicycle, and raising the funds, training and finishing this 275-mile ride through the hills of New England was the toughest challenge I have faced in my life, but I did it with a new awareness.

Michael is still the same person I love and admire. His revelation did not change him—it changed me.

## ANALYSIS

In this essay, the author tackles a controversial subject—homosexuality—in an honest and humane way. Through describing his close friendship, he reveals himself to be a compassionate and loyal person, open to new perspectives and willing to adapt to and learn about the needs and feelings of those around him.

The essay has two main strengths: its clear narrative structure and its direct, confident writing style. The author tells the story of his friendship with Michael without trying to add complexity to the issues involved. He starts by explaining what their friendship means to him; recounts the most significant moment in the friendship and how he dealt with it, and concludes with how his friendship has become stronger as a result. It is not a new story, but that it is told without pretense makes it fresh and readable, and makes us like its author. The vocabulary is not highfalutin and the sentence structure is as simple as can be. As a result, the author appears genuine and nothing gets in the way of the emotions being expressed.

Of course, the essay could be improved. For one, the author could have added a good bit more detail about his friendship with Michael without compromising the simple and direct style. Instead, many sentences are too general to have a lasting impact on the reader and sound a bit clichéd (e.g., "Our relationship has become stronger, and we know that nothing will ever come between us.") More curiously, the author spends too many words in the second paragraph describing and, indeed, praising his own personality. Though he starts off the paragraph well, explaining what he and Michael had in common, we are left to wonder what the extensive self-description adds to the story of his friendship. In total, however, the essay is a winner precisely because of its overall honesty and its prevailing lesson of selflessness.

—Geoffrey C. Upton

# "A Mixture"

By Anjanette Marie Chan Tack, who attended a small public school in
Pointe-à-Pierre, Trinidad and Tobago.

*They will send the Indians to India,*
*Send the Africans to Africa,*
*Well, somebody please just tell me*
*Where they're sending poor me, poor me?*
*Because I'm neither one or the other,*
*Six of one, half a dozen of the other,*
*I really don't know what will happen for true,*
*They're bound to split me in two!*

—"The Mighty Dougla"[1]
Popular Calypso

The dilemma this "dougla"[2] faces in this song parallels what many
people experience when meeting me for the first time. With a last
name like "Chan Tack," they envision a pure Chinese. On being con-
fronted with the flesh, however, they are invariably surprised to see
coffee-brown skin, black-brown curly hair, full lips and a small nose. It
is only the trademark Chinese eyes that give any ring of veracity to my
claim to a Chinese surname.

Being a mixture of many ethnicities: East Indian, Chinese, Spanish,
Portuguese and unidentifiable other, I believe that I am an embodi-
ment of the "melting pot" that my country, Trinidad, proudly claims to

[1] The calypsonian's sobriquet. (A calypsonian is a singer of a certain type of
Trinidadian music called calypso.)
[2] Trinidadian colloquialism for children of mixed, especially East Indian and
African, descent.

be. Living in a country as ethnically and hence culturally diverse as Trinidad and Tobago, and being myself a blend of cultures, has been one of the most significant influences in my life.

Trinidadian[3] society is not racially discriminating, but racially polarized. However, inter-race relations are generally harmonious. Fortunately, I live in a very supportive environment. Despite this, I have often had to field questions like "Anjie, what are you?" This, at first, made me feel uncomfortable. The fact that people were attempting to dissect and qualify who I was disturbed me. I was a "what," not a "who"—an oddity, it seemed. However, I soon realized that these questions were generally not malicious. They were simple expressions of the curiosity of people who were intrigued by my "different"-ness.

Throughout my childhood, "what" I was was never really an issue. As far as I was concerned, my family and friends loved me—the whole person. Today, it is not really an issue, but it has, in fact, affected me most profoundly.

My colorful ethnic heritage has given me a unique perspective of life and of people of different races and religions. My participating in Divali, the Hindu festival of lights, attending Indian weddings and learning to eat rice with chopsticks are all heartwarming and indelible experiences. Such participation in the traditions of the myriad ethnicities of my cultural heritage has left me with little room for any sort of prejudice against others. My experience has thus made me much more open-minded and nonjudgemental towards people. It has also whetted my appetite to learn about other cultures and hence has fostered in me an intense desire to travel in order to experience the lifestyles of different peoples. I feel equipped to respect divergent beliefs although I may not understand them. Most of all, I know that the value of a person can only be assessed in his/her entirety.

---

[3] A citizen of the Republic of Trinidad and Tobago.

Some people say that being mixed means that one has no roots, no identity. On the contrary, I have found that my heritage gives me roots branching out in all directions—it does not limit, but rather, enriches the quality of my life and my experiences.

## ANALYSIS

Chan Tack's essay is typical of those where the writer discusses identity—what they identify themselves with, their ethnic and racial background, and how their identity has affected their relations with others. In this case, the writer explores her identity in relation to her friends: "I was a 'what' not a 'who'—an oddity, it seemed." Essays of this type can explore experiences with discrimination, a new culture, or how a person's identity has influenced their actions.

This piece effectively conveys to the reader Chan Tack's thoughts on her mixed heritage. We see how she has come to terms with her background by dealing with poignant questions such as "Anjie, what are you?" We can imagine people asking this quite innocently. Fortunately, Chan Tack definitively says that she has grown from her experiences and has risen above the superficial characteristics that caused her friends to ask such questions. She keeps a positive outlook, showing that she has learned and grown from her experiences.

The quotation in the beginning of the essay could have been used more throughout the piece. There might have been more closure to the essay if the quotation had been referred to throughout. Was she "split in two"? How did she overcome these forces? If you include a quotation, be sure to explain and develop it wholly and completely. Don't just stick in an eloquent quotation unless it adds considerably to your piece and is one of the building blocks of your essay. Likewise, to write an effective essay, it is very important for the writer to explain all the statements made throughout the piece. Chan Tack mentions that she "lives in a very supportive environment," but does not illustrate to the reader why this is so. Including a more detailed account of an experience in which her racial background played an important role would have illustrated exactly how Chan Tack came to realize that her heritage "enriches the quality of [her] life."

—Daniel A. Shapiro

# "Tears and Fears"

By Meaghan Beattie, who was homeschooled in Oakland, California.

My sister and I have never had a fight that lasted longer than an afternoon. Once the anger had faded, we simply forgot that there had been anything to fight about (which there probably wasn't to begin with). New acquaintances might assume that our mostly peaceful relationship comes as a result of our newfound maturity, but I suspect it stems from a connection that began many years ago.

I have heard stories of my response to hearing that I would have a sibling. Evidently, it's lucky that Katherine is a girl, for my desire for a baby sister to play with excluded any possibility of a brother. At the ripe old age of two, I am rumored to have declared, "If it's a boy, we'll just have to flush it down the toilet."

Yes, I can't imagine having any sibling other than Katherine. We seem so different to an outside observer, but in some ways, we're so alike it's scary. We know exactly how to make each other laugh, because we have the same sense of humor. Sometimes we'll even blurt out the exact same sentences. As we mature, it seems we're learning how to appreciate each other more than we ever could before.

This deepening in our understanding of each other came in part as a result from the frightening and intangible illness that took hold of Katherine two years ago. It started with a constant fear of brushing people, when she was feet away. It then regressed to compulsive hand washing, and finally to the fear that everything that wasn't freshly washed, that had been outside the house, was contaminated. When I came home from my classes at Merritt, I had to change out of my clothes and shoes in the garage, since they were contaminated. She sat on towels and walked around wrapped in a clean blanket so that she wouldn't touch any of the dirty furniture.

But what frightened me more than all of these rules was what happened when the rules were not obeyed. There would be screaming in the middle of the night, when the monster in her brain told her she had touched something dirty. At first, my immaturity led me to believe that she had some sort of control over this, that it was some kind of play for attention. After all, she has always been the drama queen of the family. But I soon realized how painful it was for her to see how badly our mom hurt, and then I knew that she had fallen victim to a parasite of the mind. How terrifying it must be, to lose control over your own thoughts.

Throughout the whole ordeal, the moment that scared me the most was when my mom, sobbing, made me promise never to let Kath end up in an institution. How could my baby sister, the one who used to make up 20-minute Christmas carols for the camcorder, ever end up in a place like that? She'll be far too busy for that, what with becoming a movie star, owning a candy store, and designing her own clothing line. But beyond that, how could anyone, especially my mom, think that I would let her end up locked away?

I can remember one afternoon, Mom needed to go out to buy groceries, so Kath and I were home alone together for the first time since her illness took over. We sat outside in the sun, she was wrapped in a towel, writing her first soon-to-be bestseller, *The Littlest O'Rally,* while I sat playing solitaire. She looked up, we talked, and we cried. At a time when I understood so little about what was happening to my little Kath, I seemed to be getting to know her on a deeper level, witnessing her strength, sensing that we shared some of the same hidden fears.

Maybe that's what makes our bond so unbreakable now, knowing that we can make it through anything together. I had to grow up quickly during that brief period of time; we all did. Now that Kath is receiving treatment, and starting to regain control over her brain, I don't think I'll ever be prouder of her than I am right now. And sometimes, when we're on the road, forced to share a bed, I'll watch her sleep, lips parted, cheeks flushed, and I'll smile, content in the knowledge that my little hero can conquer anything.

## ANALYSIS

This essay works by portraying the overwhelming impact of a single individual—in this case a younger sister—on the life of the author. Although a sibling's influence can sometimes be a hackneyed subject, here it edges on controversy by introducing the reader to the poignancy of mental illness. Because this is such an obviously sensitive and personal topic, it must be undertaken with an appropriate amount of discretion on the part of the author, who must take care to not come across as too sensational or insincere. Here, the author's execution of the topic does indeed ensure its integrity and readability.

The levity of the essay's opening contrasts with its somber theme but works particularly well in slowly captivating the reader. In the first few paragraphs, we get an overview of Meaghan's interactions with her sister—all of which use thoughtful details that shed light on the author's personality and bring a smile to the reader's face.

The steady progression of the narrative shifts in the third paragraph when Meaghan begins to reflect on the difficulties of dealing with her sister's mental illness. The five emotional paragraphs that follow have a lasting impact on the reader more for their heartrending content than for their rhetoric or language.

In fact, the pathos of the story is so powerful that the author's rambling and informal language can get distracting and even frustrating. If the strength of this essay lies in its honesty and smooth style, its weakness is definitely in its diction, stream of consciousness, and lack of organization. Perhaps these problems could have been alleviated if the author had toned down some of her informal language (like "ripe old age of two" and "Yes, I can't imagine") and spent more time elaborating on a specific moment in her struggle to face her sister's illness. Writing several paragraphs on the afternoon she spent with her sister might have better focused Meaghan's observations to create a more coherent piece.

Overall, the emotion and sincerity that lie at the heart of this narrative make it interesting to read while also highlighting the author's loyalty and caring. Ultimately, Meaghan is not merely a name at the top of a page, but a real person with an experience that an admissions officer would remember.

—Kimberly A. Kicenuik

# "Two Good Friends"

By Paul S. Gutman, who attended a private school in Dallas, Texas.

In the last year and a half, I have lost two good friends. In sixty years, only two departed friends might be a blessing, but I have plenty of time in my future to worry about death and mourning.

On the last day of my 1994 spring break, I came downstairs to hear: "Paul, Dan is dead." I could not comprehend: my friend wasn't sick; in fact, I had seen him two days earlier. We had both stayed at the same hotel in Florida. How could someone nearly my age be dead? He had been killed in a jet-skiing accident. This summer, my parents called me at Georgetown. Without much preamble, my mom told me that Jack, Dan's father, had died. On his way to a dinner, Jack had collapsed from a heart attack.

In the spring of 1994, Dan had been anxious to try jet skiing. I, too, wanted to jet ski, but I found myself too busy qualifying for SCUBA certification to accompany him. Before I left Florida, I waved goodbye to him from a sunny beach. I promised to see him in a few months. Four days later, I visited with a tearful family in cold, wet, dreary New York. The death shocked Dan's friends, and all were in tears. Yet, I could not cry. I didn't know then, and I still don't know why that was.

As I looked into set after set of bloodshot, tear-laden eyes, I felt callous for not accepting the grief and crying. I felt reproached by each and every one of Dan's friends, despite the pain I shared with them. The pain continued to worm into my heart, and it still digs uncomfortably into me when I consider Dan's death. It was especially hard to see Dan's younger brother crying. After all, we are that age where we are supposed to be impervious and believe we are invincible. His sadness has carried over to me; I have never embraced the "I'm going to live forever" attitude, but Dan's death weighs on me because we were so close. On that spring day, I lost a good friend. He was two years my senior: the perfect age difference for a little bit of hero worship. Dan was a vivacious, loving person, and frequently wore a smile as part of his wardrobe. Jack was probably the hardest hit, and he never recovered.

Jack had been a friendly, outgoing man who had driven me to his beach house many times. He always smiled, and was always involved with his sons. At Jack's funeral this summer, I saw his family for the third time in fifteen months. Two of those times, we were in a funeral home and nobody was emotionally stable. Although I know that nobody lives forever, Jack's death troubles me because he was not much older than my father.

The night of Jack's funeral, my mother and my father were plagued by bad dreams, my dad dreaming that he himself had a heart attack. I can only hope that my mother or father does not have to suffer the same torture that Jack and Dan's family is enduring.

I endure a torture of my own: I cannot cry for these two friends— one a peer and the other an adult. Both were role models. They were fine human beings: one whom I wanted to be, and one whom I wanted to become. I want to be as well-rounded a person as Dan. I want to become the successful and happy man, Jack. Their passing hurts more because I cannot cry; the lack of tears seems to be a sort of weakness. I do, however, miss both of them, and I know that, like Jay McInerny writes in *Brightness Falls*, missing someone is a way of spending time with them.

## ANALYSIS

This essay is a solid attempt to describe what were obviously two very difficult times in the life of the author. While writing on such a topic is by no means the only way to show an admissions officer the maturity of your life experiences, this is a situation in which the events had a great impact on the applicant, therefore, making them appropriate subject matter for a personal statement.

The essay is especially strengthened by the amount of detail Gutman uses to describe his feelings, when he first learned that his good friend had died and the way these feelings changed as time passed. His description of attending Dan's funeral is especially good because he does not simply tell us he was sad. Gutman challenges the reader to understand and trace his grief, anger, and confusion. He repeats this when he describes the death of Dan's father, strengthening the essay even more by both drawing parallels between the two and highlighting how they impacted him differently.

Still, this essay could be improved with tighter writing and better organization, especially in the conclusion. Gutman's reference to his parents toward the end of the essay is somewhat distracting; up until that point, he had been the focal point. The transition into the last paragraph could have been better explained and established, since we do not know what helped the author accept the death of his two friends. Even more importantly, the final reference to an outside author is distracting. Gutman could have made this point on his own without allowing another author to intrude on his very personal essay.

—Georgia N. Alexakis

# "The Beast"

By Daniel Myung, who attended a public school in Lexington,
Massachusetts.

For the last seventeen years, I have been struggling to peacefully coexist with the beast residing on my scalp. This beast has been a source of great grief and pain. This beast I am talking about is my curly hair.

Because of this outstanding feature, I was treated like a mutant and a novelty by Flushing, New York's, Korean community. I was a sponge for ridicule, and the envy of every mother who permed her hair or wore mascara. (Yes, even my eyelashes curled.) From the day I picked up my first comb, I made every attempt to kill the hated billows that made my life miserable. I wanted to be like everybody else.

It was not until high school that I rethought my reason to battle the beast. I realized that my hair is a unique attribute, and that my tormentors placed my inferiority complex upon me. Killing the beast would simply show I had succeeded in correcting my "flaw" and was ready to disappear into Korean obscurity. I no longer wanted the dead and lifeless hair that everyone else had. It was time for me to discipline the untamed beast and to define who I am.

Dreadful pictures, like the one on my driver's license, are rare occurrences now, and high humidity no longer scares me. My new approach to the beast has been a great blessing. It has given me the opportunity to appreciate the beauty and versatility of the curl and to discover how living with it has defined my character. By not resigning myself to being an average, limp-locked Korean, I have always sought to put my flair, my "curliness," into all that I do. It is my desire to be the one head that always stands out. As a musician, artist, and student, my greatest fear and obstacle is anonymity.

Any cellist can read music and create pleasant noise, but not all cellists play with emotion. Skill may be present, but flavor—fire—is not. Ever since my beginning days, my playing has always had intensity and passion. This "curl" to my playing is my greatest asset, for even if my skill is lacking, my vigor makes up for it.

This same vigor is also put into my efforts to produce our school's yearbook. Our task is to produce an original, one-of-a-kind book. So many yearbooks I have seen are bland and hardly distinguishable from the next, as if only the pictures were replaced in each one. It is my mission to make our yearbook as original, witty and unique as possible.

## ANALYSIS

This essay scores points for taking a more comical approach in describing how the author overcame a major obstacle in his life—his curly hair. While the life experience described is not the most extreme example of hardship and suffering, the applicant uses humor to stand out in the minds of admissions officers and create a memorable essay.

Still, the essay suffers from a common pitfall of many admissions essays: the writer tells his story rather than illustrates it through examples. We rely on the author to tell us he was ridiculed rather than being shown through particularly humiliating scenarios in his life. Such details would have livened up the essay even more, capitalizing on its already humorous subject matter, and given the author a better opportunity to display his skills as a writer and observer.

This lack of detail becomes an even bigger problem when Myung talks about his personal transition from someone who hated his curly hair to someone who came to accept it. This was obviously a life-changing moment for the author, but all we know is that the attitude change came sometime during his high school career.

The need for clear and well-articulated transitions becomes even more important when Myung connects his accepting his physical differences to his excellence in extracurricular activities. The transition between the two subjects is abrupt and the essay ends on an abrupt note as well.

So while the choice of subject matter was original and humorous, this essay could have been made better with more examples from the author's childhood and the formative years in which he came to accept and love his "beast." Because the admissions essays are usually best when short and limited in their scope, Myung might have done better to limit his personal statement to his hair or his cello or the yearbook. Trying to link the three produces an essay with weak transitions and superficial treatment of otherwise interesting subject matter.

—Georgia N. Alexakis

# "Between a Rock and Home Plate"

By Mark K. Arimoto, who attended a medium-sized private school in Honolulu, Hawaii.

"Athlete." Often the word conjures up the image of a lithe, muscled person with one percent body fat, and able to leap tall buildings in a single bound. I am not this person. In fact, my career as an athlete is not what most consider successful. I have always enjoyed participating in athletics. Whether my ability is equal to my enthusiasm is another story.

My first sport was baseball. I was constantly trying to make up for being the smallest on the team. I would try to swing the bat as hard as my home-run-hitting teammates but my hits would invariably pop skyward or dribble weakly in the vicinity of third base. I would try to throw the ball as far as my cannon-armed fellow outfielders, only to see my coaches run forward so they could pick it up while it was still rolling. About the only thing I could do with any degree of success was run. Small but quick, I would hustle on and off the field, to and from my position, hoping to impress my coaches with my enthusiasm if not with my playing skills.

In the interim between my fifth- and sixth-grade season I worked hard. I knew it would take much more than running around to land a starting position in my final season in the Bronco division. I even attended my school's intermediate baseball tryouts a year early to improve my skills.

On the final day of the intermediate tryouts I reached out to catch a fly ball . . . and felt my thumb crush between the ball and glove. With a broken thumb I would be out for the first half of the season. My hopes for starting felt as crushed as my finger.

However, I continued to persevere and to preserve my faith and the skills I had worked so hard to improve. I read books on fielding and hitting, watched instructional videos, and sat on the sidelines cheering for my team as I waited for my finger to heal.

When at long last I could play again, I was determined to prove to the coaches and to myself that a decent ballplayer lurked in my rather unimpressive 4'10", eighty-five-pound frame. The weeks of preparation showed in my playing; I still wasn't hitting home runs and my arm still wasn't a cannon, but I would get base hits and the coaches didn't need to run forward to pick up my throws, earning a starting position at centerfield. All too soon it was the final game and we were playing for second place. More than that, we were playing against our rivals, the Yankees. We took the field with all the determination and intensity of the World Series.

The score remained close throughout the game as the ninth inning drew near. In the top of the ninth, we were tied at ten all with two outs and the Yankees' slugger at bat. An image of Mighty Casey, except with a joyous Mudville, ran through my mind as he strode to the plate. Our coaches waved a signal and the outfield played deep. I saw the pitcher slowly wind up while the Yankee behemoth waved his bat behind his head in anticipation. Then the waiting was over. The fastball headed straight for the heart of the strike zone and with a quick, tight swing I heard the crack of the bat. Far from shooting like a rocket as his other hits had, the ball was sailing in a lazy arc heading for the hole I had created by playing deep. I sprinted forward, the noise of the crowd fading in my ears as I focused on the small, falling sphere before me, hoping the drills I had practiced endlessly would help me now. As I drew nearer, I knew my legs wouldn't propel me fast enough to position myself under the ball. Without thinking, I took a final few steps and dove forward.

Rolling as I hit the ground, I jumped to my feet searching the ground for the ball. A second later I opened my glove and found the baseball nestled snugly in the pocket.

We ran off the field jumping up and down, laughing and cheering. It was the bottom of the ninth, our final time at bat for the season, and we were determined to win. Unfortunately, unlike the Yankees, our best hitters were not up to bat. We managed to advance a runner to third base, but not without the cost of two outs. Just as the Yankees had only needed a base hit to score, so did we. But whereas the Yankees had their slugger, the Braves were at the bottom of the order: me.

My hitting had not improved as much as my fielding since last season. Sensing the power in my arms, the infield positioned themselves closer. The pitcher threw the ball. I swung. Strike one! He threw again. Again I swung. Strike two! I stepped out of the batter's box. I thought about all the drills I had practiced, all the books I had read, all the videos I had watched. I thought about all the time I had sat on the sidelines waiting to play. I stepped back into the batter's box and stopped thinking about everything except my hitting drill. Step. Plant. Swing. Follow through. It echoed in my head. I saw the third pitch barrel in. I stepped. I planted. I swung. I followed through. I felt the bat connect. Not looking to see where it flew I ran faster than I ever had before. Standing on first, I turned and saw the ball in the outfield and my teammate on home plate. We had won!

After the game, the team huddled around as the coaches gave their final post-game speech. They congratulated everyone and then turned to me. I had been voted the team's MVP, and they presented me with the "game-winning rock." (The ball I had hit actually belonged to the Yankees.) A few weeks later I received a congratulatory note from my coaches. They talked of my batting average and defensive play, but I was particularly touched when they wrote, "More importantly, your enthusiasm and hustle set the tone for others. You are a natural leader and we thoroughly enjoyed being your coaches."

I realized then that it wasn't my skill so much as my spirit that earned me the rock and the respect of my coaches. I would like to go on to describe how after this incident I went on to become a star player for my school team, but to tell the truth, I was cut twice.

After my baseball endeavors, I was in ninth grade and able to try out for the tennis team. Although I was cut from my new sport two years in a row, I didn't feel badly because I had given it my best. The coach took me aside after cuts and offered me the position of manager. He had seen how I had come to every practice and had played with a lot of heart, if not a lot of skill. I was elated. For me, it was an opportunity to learn the ropes and still practice with the team. In my junior year I tried out for a sport without many cuts, paddling. Just before training went into full swing, I ruptured my tricep volunteering at a service project (making, of all things, kadomatsu, a Japanese New Year symbol of endurance, strength, and good luck). The doctors said it would take four weeks to heal, the season began in three. After talking with the coaches I continued to train with the team. I ran the three miles the team ran for conditioning, then ran another two. I lifted weights in order not to lose strength in my arms as my tricep healed. By the third week I was ready to paddle and rejoined my crew by the second race.

While the paddling team was perennially in last place, it did not detract from my experience with athletics. Indeed, this experience has given me much more than a rock, a note, and a JV letter; it has given me the confidence, strength, and motivation to persevere despite setbacks. It has shown me an inner strength, a spirit that the three "trophies" represent, a spirit born out of love for what I am doing, a spirit that doesn't let doubt and self-pity stand in the way of achieving goals, a spirit that fuels my desire to achieve.

Truly, for me, athletics has been a success, if not in the traditional sense; after all, it's not every day that one receives the game-winning rock.

## ANALYSIS

"Between a Rock and Home Plate" is an eloquently written admissions essay in which the applicant describes his trying experiences as an athlete.

Immediately pointing out that he does not fit into the mold of the stereo-typical "jock," he explains how he never let his size or lack of athletic skill stop him from following his dreams. Through each sporting experience, from Little League baseball to high school tennis, the applicant expresses his enthusiasm and desire to work hard at whatever goal he is trying to accomplish.

The strength of this essay lies in the way it is written. In particular, the precise use of adjectives gives the reader a clear picture of the applicant's struggles to make the team. Also, the use of figurative devices, such as the similes ("My hopes for starting felt as crushed as my finger") and meta-phors ("cannon-armed fellow outfielders") help solidify the reader's under-standing of the challenges the applicant faced. In turn, the reader gains a firm comprehension of the amount of enthusiasm the applicant has when going after his goals. One common admission essay problem is generality—applicants often try to explain their triumphs in a number of different areas instead of focusing on one topic. While this essay does ex-plain the applicant's determination in a variety of different sports, he does not skimp on details. Each topic gets explained fully and in depth.

The depth and description of each sport the applicant played is com-mendable; however, the essay is on the long side. The applicant could have chosen to write about either baseball or tennis, but probably should not have chosen both. The climax of the essay comes with the game-winning hit, and shortly thereafter, the essay should probably end. Another improvement might be to remove the two last paragraphs, which describe the lessons learned from sporting experiences. The goal when writing this type of essay is for the stories to express the positive traits of the applicant, without having to list them explicitly. Clearly, these stories express the ap-plicant's positive traits of determination and dedication, so it is unneces-sary to summarize them at the end.

—Joshua H. Simon

# "Learning to Fly"

By Inés Pacheco, who attended a large public high school in
Indianapolis, Indiana.

For seven weeks, I lived above a faucet shop with a pilot, a punk, a
hippie, and a traditional Galician dancer. I spent my summer in
St. Brieuc, France, studying the language with the Indiana University
Honors Program in Foreign Languages. It's a rather lengthy title for a
rather simple program. Though the goal of my study abroad was to perfect my French and learn firsthand about French culture, I found the
relationship I formed with my crazy family much more valuable.

Perhaps it was my sister Nolwennn's bright orange jumpsuit, long
hair, or her ancient clunker of a white Toyota van decorated with traditional African print curtains that really caught my attention. Or maybe
it was just that she was an hour late to pick me up when I arrived in
town in June. Actually, it was all of this that made me suddenly realize
that indeed I was in France, an ocean away from my family and friends.
My sister's looks were the complete opposite of what I had expected;
her friendliness and laughter was the only thing that kept me from
bursting into tears. When we pulled up in front of a shop with faucets
in the front windows, she announced gleefully that we were home.
Home? I had never missed my little house in the suburbs more. I met
my other sister, Poline, later that night. Though two years younger than
I, she towered over me—I barely came up to her shoulders. She wore a
black shirt with a giant red A (at first I thought she was into Nathaniel
Hawthorne, but later found out that her cause of choice was anarchy)
and baggy black pants with a belt made of bullets. Her intimidating
appearance contrasted sharply with her infectious laughter and somewhat naïve attitude. My host mother, Nicole was also somewhat different than I had expected. She had recently divorced and was
symbolically liberating herself from her failed marriage by taking flying lessons.

A few weeks after having arrived, another student came to stay. She was from Galicia in Spain and spoke barely a few words of French. I acted as a sort of translator for the month that she was a part of our family. She spoke in Spanish and I would translate her words into French. Finally, my fluency in Spanish paid off. Until last summer, I was convinced that my Venezuelan heritage and my parents' insistence that I speak Spanish would never serve me well. Because my two sisters had lives and friends of their own, Nicole took us everywhere with her. In the course of our outings we met, among other people, a minor-league soccer player, many pilots, and an eighty-six-year-old accordion player who was convinced that everyone in the American government was Jewish.

My *famille des femmes fantastiques* (as I came to know them) taught me a great deal. First, I learned that family—whether it be of actual relatives or friends—is irreplaceable. Together we learned that the perfect conclusion to a low-fat dinner was chocolate mousse. They also taught me that, contrary to popular belief, routine makes life more interesting. Every Friday we ate galettes and crepes; every Saturday we would trek to the town market and buy fresh vegetables, fruit, flowers, and meat. I loved everything about the market, save for the inevitable chopping-off of chicken heads. Nicole encouraged me to create my own routine. So I did. Every Saturday afternoon, I rode the city bus into town—and often chuckled at what I heard on the radio. It was an amusing surprise to hear middle-aged women singing along to R. Kelly or Eminem. After getting off the bus, I walked around by myself for a few hours, taking in the sights and smells of city life. After a solitary cup of coffee, I would wander into the bookstore and pick out a few books. Instead of judging books by their covers, I judged them by their titles . . . which ones sounded the best as they rolled off the tongue. *Huis Clos, L'Étranger*, and *Paroles* have such pleasant-sounding titles; I wouldn't even have had to read them to enjoy them. Then on Sunday after an informal lunch with family and friends, I chose one of my new books and sat out under the heat-wave sun and read until I had finished the whole thing.

On a whim, Nolwenn and I decided to sit in during one of Nicole's flying lessons. I didn't even think twice about getting in the back. We put on our headsets and I grabbed Nolwenn's hand for dear life until I saw the French countryside below me. It was at that moment that I recognized how far I had come. I had no problem going out by myself. I had no shame about asking for direction or clarification. I went, alone, to a rally for the liberation of José Bové, the man in jail for bulldozing various McDonalds in France. I even got into a tiny airplane despite my horrible fear of flying. I had become comfortable with myself and had learned to trust my decisions, my intuition. More importantly, I had learned to trust a group of complete strangers who became my unlikely overseas family.

## ANALYSIS

Pacheco has taken a common experience, studying abroad in the summer, and transformed it into something unique and memorable. Most essays on studying abroad focus on the perils of learning a foreign language and the barriers one must break down in order to access another culture, but this essay focuses on something more unexpected: living with a host family.

Pacheco clearly has an eye for detail and a sense of humor that she's not afraid to use. The strength of her essay lies in its vivid descriptions and humorous tone. Pacheco describes her host sister, playing on her fashion taste to make a literary quip: "She wore a black shirt with a giant red A (at first I thought she was into Nathaniel Hawthorne, but later found out that her cause of choice was anarchy) and baggy black pants with a belt made of bullets." This sentence is a good example of an effective use of humor to tell a story.

Another major strength of the essay is its structure: the writer lays out a clear trajectory to show how she has grown and the lessons she has learned. She begins with her arrival in St. Brieuc as an unhappy, scared

# Influences • 69

student, and ends with a few anecdotes of moments when she showed her newfound confidence and independence. This structure of painting a "before" or "beginning" scene to contrast with an "after" scene allows the author to document how she grew and what she learned in a very convincing manner.

A few parts of the essay could be improved. It is a bit long, and becomes digressive at times. And while most of the details are necessary, some are extraneous and could be cut. For example, we don't need to know that the eighty-six-year-old accordion player the author met thought everyone in the American government was Jewish. The writing could also be more concise and a little more precise (she should have used fewer "thens" as transitions).

Overall, however, the picture the writer paints of herself is detailed, endearing, and most importantly memorable. The writer also manages to include personal anecdotes (like about her Venezuelan parents) within an interesting story of her summer. From the first line, Pacheco immediately draws readers in with her humor and snappy writing style, and keeps them attentive and entertained throughout the essay by telling a story of a summer of learning and laughter.

—Lauren A. E. Schuker

# "My Mother's Books"

By Pat Blanchfield, who attended a small all-scholarship private high school in New York City.

A fter nineteen years of loving intimacy with my mother, I grapple with a sense that a fundamental part of her remains unapproachably alien to me.

In 1967, at the age of fifteen, my mother emigrated from Krakow, Poland, completely ignorant of English; within ten years, she had graduated as salutatorian from a Chicago ghetto high school, received a degree in architecture from IIT, and gotten her masters at Harvard. My mother votes regularly (Democratic, always), reads Maeve Binchy novels, pays no attention to sports, and cooks, and cleans, and escorts my sister to dance and swimming classes. Outwardly, my mother seems fully assimilated into American culture, her few peculiarities unremarkable within the wide boundaries of what is to be expected in pluralistic New York. On a family visit to Poland, cab drivers regularly commented on her American accent.

Nonetheless, hints at my mother's earlier identity tantalize me. Though fluent in English, my mother admittedly lacks the eloquence of a lifelong speaker, the occasional incorrect pronoun pointing, like some archaeological clue, to her foundations in an inflected language. My mother's handwriting, loopy and vertical when cursive, composed of almost-typewritten capitals when print, bears the stamp of homogenous Eastern European education, revealed equally in the style of all her Polish friends. My mother gives peaks and bases to her ones, and crosses her sevens. She eats fishes with two forks, tearing through meals with intense rapidity. On the few occasions when I have seen my mother truly angry, her pronunciation has slipped, and she has reverted to an odd Polish-English fusion.

Most of my mother's traits are endearing, and easily forgotten in the

mire of the quotidian. At times, however, aspects of my current
mother's self, manifested less against the background of her familiar
behavior than in pictures, overlooked objects and a-contextual statements, so unmistakably point to some other, radically different person,
that I am jarred. Grainy photos haunt me: my mother, petite, pale,
standing in the rain on the cobbles of some Warsaw street, her long hair
wet, smiles almost imperceptibly at me with a smile intended for my
father behind the camera. In profile, in Paris, looking out at Les In-
valides, or playing with swans in Stein Ahm Rein. She is beautiful,
lithe, a straight-haired *Casablanca* Elsa, visiting her home one step
ahead of martial law (my father is hardly a Victor Lazlo in these pictures: tall, lanky and mustachioed, he seems out of place, a little ill at
ease except in those photos where he is drinking Zubrowka with my
uncles. *His* pictures—in which incidentally, he, too, has long hair—
are of baseball and Harleys and outrageous road trips, and do not convey any sense of mystique to me, perhaps unfairly). Even in these
pictures, however, my mother seems slightly shy, burdened in what
used to be her home country by relative affluence and enthusiasm, and
an American citizenship. She has only begun to live in the limbo that I
now know her in.

My mother is uncomfortable in the language of her birth. Behind the
framed photos on our living room shelves are rows upon rows of Polish
books, somehow brought over when my mother first emigrated: Mick-
iewicz's *Pan Tadeusz*, Sienkiewicz's *Quo Vadis*, dozens of ethnic works
of fiction and non-, and, in translation demonstrative of typically Slavic
Francophilia, whole sets of Proust and Dumas. These books are tokens
of my family's once-privileged position as Krakow intelligentsia, em-
blems of a unique capacity for leisure and a devotion to scholarship.
My mother does not, practically speaking, read any of these now: years
of neglect have diminished her Polish skills such that any attempt to
enjoy her parents' literature now demands excessive effort on her part.
English is preferable, now. She no longer remembers most of her

books' plots, even those that she most favored. More troublingly, even the books that my mother enjoyed in English during her college years are vague to her. Perusing our large library, I come across a half-dozen volumes of Sartre, and ask for her recommendation: "I used to be crazy about him, and Camus also," comes her response from the kitchen, "Now I can't tell any of them apart." My mother once knew Russian, Spanish, and some German.

I am not sure whether I should ascribe the gap between my mother as I see her, coming home from work with perm askew and black blouse (designer darks have become a grotesque de facto uniform for an industry dependent on youthful style) sprinkled with gum-eraser shavings, and the straight-haired will-o'-the-wisp who gazes at me soulfully from photos to the lingering effects of cultural displacement, or to the brutally numbing progress of life. I am just as terrified by the way her Banana Republic shirt (similar in its genderlessness to so many things I wear) accentuates the dark lines around her eyes as I am affected by her occasional pause searching for words on the telephone with my taciturn grandmother—"*to jest tylko artretyzm, mamuśka.*" Ultimately, the forces that have shaped my mother's life seem to exist in inextricable duality: her triumphs in school stand as much as a function of her reaping the fruits of an ethic instilled in her by her previous foreign context as a remarkable individual's response to culturally-unspecific economic hardship, and her later difficulties in finding work in late 80's–early 90's recession-era New York are testament not only to a slightly nagging inability to forcefully articulate herself socially, and to a possible lack of self-confidence, but to her simply growing old in a profession that no longer values tenure and experience. My mother's unique experience of acclimatization to America highlights my own—and what I feel to be the transcendent—reality of maturation (I choose this word reluctantly, and deliberately avoid "growth"), while at the same time being informed by pressures which I can never appreciate. Her books, which no one now reads, are mute witnesses.

## ANALYSIS

In this essay, the author demonstrates sensitive and thoughtful reflection on his relationship with his mother. By focusing his essay on a topic that is so personal and meaningful to him, the author is able to let his own voice shine through. Writing about an influential person is a common essay question, but the author takes an approach that is perceptive and original. On the one hand, he is all too familiar with his mother's habits and quirks, providing vivid details of her handwriting, the way she eats fish, or her appearance after returning from a long day of work. At the same time, the author is captivated by the other sides to his mother that he knows so little about, both the "beautiful, lithe" woman who appears in photographs from Warsaw, and the middle-aged, outwardly assimilated woman who has experienced "pressures which I can never appreciate."

By setting up this contrast between the mother he knows and the mother he wonders about, the author finds an effective way to explore his own feelings about this figure who has played such an essential role in his life. His affection and admiration for her are evident throughout the essay, from the very first line (where he refers to their "years of loving intimacy"), to his proud inclusion of her accomplishments, to his poignant description in the last paragraph of how he worries about her. While the essay traces in large part "the forces that have shaped my mother's life," then, the author succeeds in revealing just as much about himself—which is what college admissions officers want to see.

The essay could be improved with a clearer sentence structure. For example, in the fourth paragraph, an extended parenthetical discussion of his father seems somewhat awkwardly placed, and the first sentence of the closing paragraph loses some of its rhetorical effect because it is so long. In fact, the whole essay could be trimmed, as it is pushing one thousand words. Despite these shortcomings, though, what shines through is the author's obvious love for his mother and his desire to understand her better—a goal he has likely achieved in the process of writing this candid essay.

—Jessica R. Rubin-Wills

# POINTS
# OF VIEW

# "On Diplomacy in Bright Nike Running Tights"

By Christopher M. Kirchhoff, who attended a public high school in suburban Columbus, Ohio.

B eepbeep.
    Beepbeep.

Beepbeep. With a series of subtle but relentless beeps, my faithful Timex Ironman watch alarm signaled the start of another day, gently ending the pleasant slumber I so often fail to enjoy. With the touch of a button I silenced the alarm, falling back on my bed to establish a firmer grasp of where I was and why on earth I had set my alarm for 5:45 A.M. Slowly the outline of my soundly sleeping roommate came into focus. Beyond his bed was the window. Across the Neva River the view of the Hermitage and Winter Palace, illuminated brightly with spotlights, faded in and out of the falling snow. I was definitely still in St. Petersburg, and no, this wasn't a dream. "Oh yes, running," I remembered. "Must go running."

Temperature??? I dialed the front desk. "Kakoy tempatura pozholsta." Not fooled by my Berlitz Russian, the voice responded, "Negative 7 degrees" in crisp English. I reached for my running tights, glad that meant negative seven degrees Celsius. I took another look into the darkness outside. Negative seven degrees Fahrenheit and I would not be running. The hotel lobby was empty except for the guard and the woman at the desk. As I stepped outside, I pressed the start button on my Timex Ironman and began jogging.

It was a pristine morning. The November wind promptly reminded me just what winter meant at 60 degrees north latitude. With the sky awaiting the break of dawn, I started making my way through the newly fallen snow. Soon the sound of my labored breathing came through the rhythmic swooshing of running shoes dancing through the snow. As clouds of breath collected in front of me, I passed slowly through them, marking my forward progress with each exhale. Around the corner I found a freshly shoveled sidewalk. Following the inviting path, I soon came upon the shoveler, an old man sporting the classic Russian winter outfit: fur cap, long coat, and mittens. Time had left its mark on his wrinkled face and worn clothing. Despite the falling snow, which accumulated at a far greater pace than the man could keep up with, he continued to shovel relentlessly, barely glancing up as I jogged by him. I respect his perseverance. He was working fiercely in the Russian spirit. And as the war medals proudly displayed on his coat indicate, he had been doing so for a while. Perhaps this man was one of the few that survived the Nazi siege on Leningrad, a living reminder of why the United States must remain deeply involved in world politics.

As I turned and ran across the bridge leading downtown, the battleship *Potemkin* came into view. The *Potemkin* began the second Russian Revolution by training its guns on the Winter Palace. Still afloat as a working museum, young sailors in full military dress cleared its decks of snow. While I ran past the ship, a sailor stopped to wave. As his inquisitive eyes stared into mine, we both recognized each other's young age. I waved back, shouting, "Doebroyah ootra," wishing him a good morning. A few seconds later I glanced back, noticing that the same sailor was still looking at me. I must have been quite a sight in my brightly colored Nike running suit treading through a foot of new snow. "How ironic," I thought, "here stands a high school aged Russian sailor shoveling snow off a ship which I studied in history class, while each of us is equally bewildered at the other's presence."

By the time I reached the Hermitage the sky was clear enough to see my reflection in the cold black of the Neva River. While running past the Winter Palace, I quickened my pace, half expecting the Tsarina to step out and stop my progress. I sprinted through Revolution Square, glancing left to see the spot where Tsar Nicolas abdicated and right to see the monument commemorating the defeat of Napoleon. While trodding through historic St. Petersburg, I reflected on the last discussion I had with Sasha, my Russian host student. Sasha, top in his class in the "diplomatic" track of study, had talked about his political beliefs for the first time. What begun as a question-and-answer session about life in the United States became a titanic struggle between political ideals. Sasha's tone and seriousness clearly indicated that our discourse was not for pleasure. He wanted to know about our government and what democracy meant for him and his people. Being the first U.S. citizen Sasha had ever met, I felt obligated to represent my country as best I could. Realizing that my response could forever shape his impression of democracy in the U.S., the importance of my mission as a student ambassador became even more apparent.

For Russians, democracy remains a new and untrusted method of government. Clearly, Russia is still in a state of change, vulnerable to the forces of the past and skeptical of the future. Sasha, unable to share my faith in the democratic political process, listened patiently to my explanations. I tried my best to help Sasha conceptualize what the United States is about and just what it means to be an American. For the sake of both countries I hope he accepted my pro-democracy arguments. It was conversations like these that brought a new sense of urgency to my time in Russia. Through the course of my visit, Sasha and I came to know each other and each other's people. His dream of serving as a diplomat may very well materialize. Perhaps someday Sasha will be in a position to make decisions that affect the United States. I hope my impression will in some way affect his judgment in a positive manner.

After jogging up the hotel steps, I pressed the stop button. Not bad for a morning run I thought. Sixty-four minutes in deep snow, about seven miles' worth. Press Mode button. Time zone one: E.S.T. Columbus, Ohio. It was Saturday night back home. Thinking of home, I remembered the student in my homeroom who cried, "You mean you're gonna go and meet those Commies? So you think you can change the world?" Press Mode button.

Time zone two: St. Petersburg, Russia, November 4, 1995. Greeting the dawn of a new day I thought, "Perhaps! Perhaps in some small way I can change the world, one conversation at a time."

## ANALYSIS

The month that Christopher Kirchhoff spent in Russia as a "student diplomat" undoubtedly provided him with more than enough experiences to include in an admissions application. But in his essay "On Diplomacy in Bright Nike Running Tights," Kirchhoff successfully avoids falling into the trap of many applicants whose statements are based on once-in-a-lifetime opportunities.

Kirchhoff easily could have written something along the lines of, "My time in Russia provided me with a rare opportunity to witness an emerging democracy grappling with its newfound freedom. Armed with a keen interest in the post-Communist plight, I set forth to learn from my Russian brethren and to teach them about their American peers." These statements are not necessarily untrue, but they are also not especially original. Such an essay would hardly stand out among a stack of statements written by students retelling the glory of winning the state debate/football/academic challenge championship.

Instead, Kirchhoff tells the admissions committee about the Russia he has come to know on his early-morning jogs. We learn that he is a disciplined runner, a perceptive observer of human nature, a willing learner of the Russian language. Bright Nike running tights, his Timex Ironman, and the rhythmic swooshing of his running shoes are details that his audience will remember. They also provide the perfect segue into the more substantive issues Kirchhoff wants to address in his essay—the conversations he has had with Russians his age. The reader gets to know Kirchhoff before we get to know his views on such weightier subjects as diplomacy and the American role in international relations.

While his supposedly verbatim thoughts after waving to the young sailor sound stilted ("How ironic . . . each of us is equally bewildered at the other's presence"), Kirchhoff's understated and personal approach throughout the majority of his essay makes up for his waxing a bit too eloquent at times. Ideally, it would have been nice to hear just as much detail about his conversations with Sasha as we do about St. Petersburg at 6 A.M. The essay loses the details when it matters most. Also in terms of detail, Kirchhoff makes a slight error in his statement that "the *Potemkin* began the second Russian Revolution by training its guns on the Winter Palace." It was in fact the *Aurora* that fired mostly blank rounds on the palace—the battleship *Potemkin* was the scene of a 1905 revolt by sailors in Odessa. These mistakes are rather minor since the essay is not particularly centered on the ship. However, let this serve as a valuable lesson: it is important to extensively check all facts used in your essay.

Still, Kirchhoff's essay works.

—Georgia N. Alexakis

# "The Magic of Magic"

By Harrison R. Greenbaum, who attended a mid-sized public school in Cedarhurst, New York.

I'd love to demonstrate for you the feelings I'll be describing in the coming paragraphs. You'll need this box below:

| | | | |
|---|---|---|---|
| **an** | <u>the</u> | <u>a</u> | <u>I</u> |
| <u>me</u> | **you** | **be** | **he** |
| <u>them</u> | **she** | <u>it</u> | <u>his</u> |
| <u>mine</u> | **her** | **yours** | to |

*(As originally submitted, this was in color with the words in red and blue type.)*

I would like you to concentrate on any underlined word. Think about it, visualize it, and place your finger on it (don't worry—I won't look). This has been a free choice, one I could not possibly predict. I'd like you to make another unpredictable, free choice by moving your finger left or right until you hit a word in boldface type. Let's make this more interesting and randomize the outcome further. Would you please move your finger up or down to the nearest underlined word? Let's make this really impossible now—move your finger again, but this time diagonally, in any direction, to the nearest word in boldface. Finally (we're almost there!) move your finger right or down to the nearest underlined word. Concentrate on it. Wait a second! I believe that that's what you're doing right now. Concentrating on "it."

Right now (hopefully) you're experiencing a moment of astonishment. If you are like the hundreds of spectators I've entertained as a magician, you are probably asking yourself, "How did he do that?" Those are five simple words I have heard over and over again, the universal response to any stimulus that does not fit into the boundaries of perceived reality. Although the outside observer might believe that the question is posed to me about my methodology, I know that the five words call into question everything that the witness to the magic had conceived was possible and impossible. But even though I am often asked the "How" question, I have never been asked the "Why." It is this question I would like to answer.

"Why do I do that?" I should probably start by explaining why I became a magician. Magic combines everything I love and requires everything I have to offer. Magic is one of the most intellectual of the arts, requiring creative solutions to creative problems. It is a performance art that requires stage presence and the ability to socialize with people. It requires reading and studying, playing and experimenting. Magic can be improvised or scripted, can stand alone or be incorporated into a routine. It requires dedication and practice, even when most of the products of this labor are never seen by anyone. Magic must be a passion, a part of a person, in order to be performed as it should. The magician is the sum of a great number of parts.

So why do I do it? What's the point? When does a card trick stop being a card trick? I perform magic to give what I believe is one of the most precious gifts I can give to others—the gift of astonishment. I am, in the words of Paul Harris, as he wrote in his magnum opus, *The Art of Astonishment,* "an astonishment guide." Performing magic forces the spectators to re-evaluate their pre-established conceptions and beliefs. I strive to demonstrate that people should be more open to others and others' ideas. I strive to demonstrate that nothing is impossible. I strive to demonstrate that real magic occurs around us everywhere, every day. I endeavor to pass on to people the teachings that the practitioners of this great art have been giving people since the beginning of time, from cavemen to shaman to wizards to modern-day magicians. So, why do I do it? Because life itself is magical; it is magic within and upon itself, inherently. That is why I do magic and why magic is a major part of what I am—because showing someone magic is so magical itself.

## ANALYSIS

Greenbaum's essay is immediately striking because it's creative and different. Complete with a colorful chart, it invited the reader in the Harvard Admissions Office to actually participate in what Greenbaum is describing. Everyone who reads this essay is going to follow the instructions in the first paragraph, and end up exactly where Greenbaum says they will be: concentrating on the word "it" and probably a bit surprised. This being Harvard, the admission official is also likely to try to figure out the logic behind the "magic" and, of course, realize that the essay's series of instructions all end on the same square.

In explaining why magic is to him more than just entertainment or a hobby, Greenbaum conveys the personal qualities that he considers important and that he strives to inculcate in others and himself. Magic, through his essay, becomes a stand-in for the virtues of creativity, open-mindedness, preparation and hard work, intellectual exploration, and maintaining positive relations with other people. Dropping in the title of a book that he has read on magic, Paul Harris's *The Art of Astonishment*, is a good way for Greenbaum to make clear that he takes magic seriously and considers it an intellectual endeavor.

The first section is also entertaining stylistically; just as the example trick attempts to let readers in on the thrill Greenbaum feels at figuring magic out, his choice of prose conveys his excitement when actually performing it. By writing as if he were actually speaking and administering the trick to an audience, Greenbaum sets the stage for his later discussion of how magic builds his interpersonal skills and presence.

As he moves into the more serious part of the essay, though, Greenbaum's style is at times repetitive and awkward. He unnecessarily repeats some variant on the question "Why do I do it?" multiple times; throughout the essay, he relies too heavily on rhetorical questions. Similarly, he resorts to clichés at times, particularly in the last two or three sentences as he tries to move beyond his own personal experiences with magic to make a statement about its broader meaning. The essay is best where it deals more specifically with what Greenbaum gets out of magic, and what he hopes his particular audiences will, as well.

—Elisabeth S. Theodore

# "The End Is Where We Start From"

By Evan Henry Jacobs, who attended a small private school in Annapolis, Maryland.

Working on the yearbook this summer, the other editors and I found a quote by T. S. Eliot: "What we call the beginning is often the end. And to make an end is to make a beginning. The end is where we start from." We liked it, and decided to use it on the first and last pages of the book. However, I have since come to understand these words not just in the simple context of the beginning and end of our yearbook. These words, I now realize, can be applied to my entire senior year, fraught with the complexities of college applications and the inevitable breakup of my senior class.

I understood, as my senior year started, that the year would end in June, and that by September the forty-eight members of the Key School Class of 2004 would be forever separated, scattered to dozens of colleges across the nation and to dozens of new lives. But once we started applying to colleges, and more importantly, once some of us began to set our hearts on certain schools and some of us began to get into those schools, I saw T.S. Eliot's words a little more clearly. "What we call the beginning is often the end." Our senior year officially ends June 11, but in many ways, it ended with the beginning of the college admissions process. It ended when people who once wore blue Key School shirts and sweatpants started to instead wear clothing of a different color and bearing a different name.

Yet there is more to the quote by Eliot: "To make an end is to make a beginning." Certainly, most of my classmates and I will be sad to see our class slowly breaking apart as we prepare for college. We have all learned a lot at Key, not just about academics, but about ourselves and our friends. It has been our second home. But I have been at this school for eight years now; some of my friends have been here for fourteen years. We have gotten what we can from it, and it is time to move on. For that is what the end of our senior year really is: an opportunity to move on to bigger and better things, and an opportunity to part with our old friends on good terms.

"The end is where we start from," said T.S. Eliot. I now understand that my senior year is ending, not in September, not in June, but now, as the class of 2004 begins to look out from Annapolis and see a new world to explore. I want to enjoy my time at Key as much as possible, and I will continue to do that as the year progresses. But like so many other students I have seen drift away, I am ready for a new environment, a new class to be a part of, a new adventure.

## ANALYSIS

There are two main elements to this essay that make it effective. One is the language of inclusiveness. The writer starts out immediately by stating that it was he and his editors, not he alone, who found the quote that forms the backbone of the rest of the paper. In the same way, the essay continues by speaking about the senior class as a whole, rather than only the writer himself. The fact that he points out that everyone, not just he, is going through a process of departure and discovery shows him to be someone who understands and empathizes with those around him. It also points to a humble recognition of being part of something bigger than himself, of being able to look beyond the narrow scope of senior year to what lies ahead. This is the second effective element. The admissions office seeks to admit mature students who have the potential for broad horizons. This essay says, clearly and insightfully, that the writer is that type of person.

That having been said, there is one very important element the writer could have used to improve the essay: personal information. Apart from the fact that he works on the yearbook (a fact we would have discovered from his list of extra-curricular activities anyway), we know very little about him. Perhaps he could have spoken about why Harvard was the school he set his heart on, what exactly he has learned about his friends, or what kind of adventure he hopes to experience now that senior year is ending. There are many opportunities in this essay to share something about his personality, and he neglects to do so.

It's risky to base an essay, especially a short essay, on a quote. Although this student did so successfully, it's often difficult to find the right balance between analysis and insight, speaking as yourself instead of speaking for the poet. If you do attempt it, make sure, as this student has, that the quote is the backbone of the essay, not the body itself.

—Jayme J. Herschkopf

# "Introducing Clark Kent and Willy Wonka"

By Daniel G. Habib, who attended a small Catholic high school in New York City.

My childhood passions oscillated between two poles: St. Catherine's Park and the 67th Street branch of the New York Public Library. Located across Sixty-seventh Street from one another, the two crystallized the occupations of my youth. On a typical day, I moved between a close-knit group of friends at the park to largely solitary stays at the library. My recreational pursuits were communal; my intellectual pursuits were individual. The gulf was pronounced: friends rarely joined my mother and me as we meandered among the stacks, and the books I obtained from the library never accompanied me to the basketball courts or the jungle gym. Generally, I slipped away from the park during a lull in the action and returned as stealthily as I had gone, foisting Roald Dahl paperbacks on my mother and scrambling to rejoin my friends in arguing the relative merits of the Hulk and Superman. I never thought to integrate these passions; they remained firmly segregated. That Clark Kent and Willy Wonka should never cross paths was a given; the giants existed in separate realms of my life.

More than anything else, my Regis career has reversed that assumption. I now recognize that my intellectual growth and my peer community are inextricably linked. I have come to regard those who surround me not simply as a network of friends, but most vitally as components in the ongoing work of education. I understand that an individualized process of learning is intellectually impoverished.

The most startling of my educational epiphanies have occurred in the context of fellow students. Case in point: my acquaintance with Albert Camus' absurdist manifesto, *The Stranger*. My first reading of the classic, in sixth grade, came in an atomized intellectual climate. As a result, my understanding of Camus' philosophy was tenuous, so much so that, feeling incapable of defending or even articulating my interpretation of the work, I eschewed any discussion and shunned the chance for error. Satisfied in my ignorance, I disdainfully explained to my inquiring parents, "Oh, it wasn't much of a murder mystery. You know who kills the Arab all along. And that whole mother angle just doesn't fit." My second encounter with Camus came in my junior French IV elective, this time in the company of an insightful octet of Francophones. As we grappled with Camus' vision of the absurd world and Meursault's statement of revolt, an understanding emerged from the sun-drenched Algerian beach. Each member of the class offered his insights for consideration, risking the scrutiny of the group but confident in its intellectual generosity. The rigorous standards of the class, and our common desire for understanding, led eventually to firmer comprehension. My balanced interpretation of Camus derived only from the intensity of discussion, the contributions of my peers, and our mutual willingness to share our insights.

Through my participation in Regis' Speech and Debate Society, I have continued in my quest for the acquisition of knowledge through the group. Extemporaneous Speaking requires that a speaker provide a thorough analysis of a current events/policy proposition, after considering and synthesizing numerous sources. Speakers engage each other on subjects ranging from democratic and free-market reforms in Boris Yeltsin's Russia to the prospects for a Medicare overhaul in the Republican Congress. Practices involve evaluation by fellow team members and success depends intimately on an accurate common understanding of the issues. Lincoln-Douglas Debate, similarly, entails team formulations of argument based on philosophical principles. We prepare as a team, and I have been privileged to benefit from teammates' sophisticated applications and elucidations of issues as diverse as social contract theory and international ethical mandates.

The group character of the team's intellectual strivings was brought to bear most strongly at the Harvard Invitational, in the winter of my

junior year. Debaters were asked to evaluate the proposition that
"American society is well-served by the maintenance of a separate
culture for the deaf." The evening before the tournament began, sixteen debaters massed in one hotel room at the Howard Johnson's on
Memorial Drive, and, fueled by peanut butter and marshmallow
sandwiches and gallons of coffee, we wrangled over the specifics of
the unique resolution. The assimilationist camp suggested that the
achievement of group dignity and a private identity for the deaf had
to occur against the backdrop of a larger public identity. The sepa-
ratism inherent in ASL or deaf schools fatally divorced the group from
meaningful participation in the American democracy. True cultural
uniqueness required a common frame of reference. Conversely, the
deaf separatist partisans maintained that this decidedly marginalized
minority deserved a distinctness of culture commensurate with the
distinctness of its experience. Separation allowed dignity and empow-
erment.

As the hours wore on and the dialectic raged out of control, posi-
tions became more entrenched, but paradoxically a truer comprehension arose. The eloquence and persuasiveness with which each side
advanced its interpretation furthered the exchange. We acknowledged
and respected the logic of those with whom we disagreed, and we rein-
forced our own convictions by articulating and defending them. At
1:30, bedraggled, exhausted, and happily not unanimous in perspective, we regretfully dispersed to our rooms, to sleep off the effects of the
session.

If I began my educational career as an intellectual monopolist, I
have evolved into a collectivist. On our last day of summer vacation, a
dozen Regis students spent an afternoon in the Yankee Stadium
bleachers, arguing the possible outcomes of the American League pen-
nant race, then returned to Manhattan's Central Park to attend the New
York Shakespeare Festival's arresting and hyper-controversial production of *Troilus and Cressida*. As we exited the Delacorte Theater, we re-

flected on the modernization of Shakespeare's message. Some praised its transmission of bleakness and pessimism; others joined critics in attacking its excesses and its artistic license in manipulating the original. Our consensus on the Bronx Bombers' chances in October was firmer than that on the Greek conquest of Troy, but the essential truth remains. Regis has wonderfully fused the communal and the intellectual phases of my life.

## ANALYSIS

Writing about an outstanding learning experience is a fairly common approach to the personal statement. But while many applicants may choose a defining and distinct moment—winning the state speech tournament or setting the school record for the highest GPA—as an experience worth retelling, Habib instead chooses to chronicle the gradual process of intellectual maturation. By choosing this topic, Habib has the opportunity to reflect on his education and recount several formative experiences, not just resort to trite descriptions of winning or losing.

Habib's thesis—that one's communal life and intellectual pursuits are only enhanced when fused together—is a somewhat abstract and difficult argument to make, at least for a high school senior. The fact that Habib makes the argument successfully, through the use of details and concrete examples, makes the essay all the more impressive.

Still, the essay isn't perfect. It's long. The sentences can be complex and a bit convoluted. The language used, while enough to impress any Kaplan SAT instructor, could be toned down to make the essay more reader-friendly. Habib could have easily shortened his statement by using fewer examples of real-life learning experiences. Or the experiences he shares could have been shortened: the admissions committee may not need to know the exact arguments and counter-arguments Habib's Lincoln-Douglas debate team drafted for the Harvard tournament.

Overall, Habib's essay helps distinguish him from other applicants by taking an interesting approach to a common theme and using concrete supporting arguments. All in all, it is a well-written essay enhanced by personal insights, examples, and the all-important details.

—Georgia N. Alexakis

# "Vietnamese Soup"

By Michaela N. de Lacaze, who attended a small private international
school in Paris, France.

The aromas of cilantro and ginger permeate the warm air. The vapor
of boiling broth disappears into the low pink ceiling, while ciga-
rette smoke periodically dances around paintings of pandas and bam-
boo. The hum of babbled Vietnamese and clattering plates muffle my
confident, seven-year-old request for "more lime please." My brother
is poking the plastic tablecloth with a toothpick. This is the scene trig-
gered in my mind every time I hear the phrase Vietnamese Soup—a
dish that has come to symbolize my growing up.

One Sunday when I was three, my family and I stumbled upon a
Vietnamese restaurant unknown to most people in Montreal. We returned many times to feast on our new favorite meal, the Pho Vietnamese Soup. What was at first a family's culinary caprice soon became a
family tradition. Every Sunday lunch from that time on consisted of a
bowl of Vietnamese soup, either prepared in the restaurant or at home.

What might seem to others as a finicky family's idiosyncrasy was, in
fact, a reflection of our cultural diversity. I am a Peruvian who was
raised in the French language, a Canadian who traveled in Europe, a
French citizen who made friends in Latin America, and an American
who learned English in the fifth grade. The exoticness of the Vietnamese soup epitomized this kaleidoscopic background. With the years,
however, the soup began to represent much more. At times, our constant expatriations were discombobulating. Yet, we maintained a sense
of identity and of home by keeping a few things constant. The weekly
soup tradition symbolized the inner stability and immutable bonds of
our family. We had no fixed home, set of friends, or school, but we always had our Vietnamese soup meals.

In Kentucky, where there was no Vietnamese restaurant, we cooked the soup at home in our muggy kitchen. My mother crushed the herbs, my father chopped the meat, and I placed the chopsticks and porcelain bowls on the table, while my brother doodled on the fogged windows with the tips of his fingers. In Uruguay and the Dominican Republic, the tradition continued. It was a way for us to spend time together and just talk, whether about life or my father's latest coup in smuggling Vietnamese rice noodles from Brazil. During these talks, I voiced my opinions without fear of harsh criticism or false appraisal. It would only be a matter of time before I debated in class and wooed the student body with my student council "political" speeches.

When I went by myself to work with architects in Paris, I still ate the soup. After having wandered through the Musée d'Orsay or gone to my art lessons, I systematically went to a little Vietnamese restaurant I had proudly discovered, this time without my parents. There, in the empty restaurant, I chatted with the owner's wrinkled wife, and paid the bill with my own earnings. Ironically, the family soup had become a mark of my growing independence. Even during summer school, I would eat the dish to celebrate my self-sufficiency and appease my occasional pangs of homesickness.

I still have Vietnamese soup with my family every Sunday. And each time I breathe in the smell of the cilantro and ginger, I remember how much I have changed and yet, not changed, since those childhood days of babbled Vietnamese and clattering plates.

## ANALYSIS

This is a very nice essay in which the author uses her family's favorite dish as a metaphor for her identity, arguing that the blending of the soup's ingredients aptly describes her own cultural diversity. Rather than representing the flux and instability of her constant relocation, however, the dish adopts the opposite meaning as a symbol of stability within her family. The applicant makes the somewhat standard technique of using an experience or an object to reflect upon a broader character trait more interesting by subtly weaving in some of her other interests, such as her student council involvement and her art lessons. This technique is highly effective and allows her essay to tie together several activities likely explained elsewhere in her application.

The author does a wonderful job of engaging her readers' senses. After opening with a vivid description of the Vietnamese restaurant, it closes by alluding to the same "clattering plates." Parts of the essay, however, seem a bit fragmented; several sentences and ideas, such as her growing independence and leadership training, stick out as a bit detached from the focus on the paragraph. If she had crafted seamless transitions between these ideas, or perhaps focused on fewer episodes, the piece would flow more smoothly.

—Jessica E. Vascellaro

# "History as Calculus"

By Jesse Field, who attended a selective state-run math and science college-level program in San Antonio, Texas.

As far back as I can remember, I have wanted to be a scientist. Lately I have done a lot of thinking about what divides sciences like physics and mathematics, slowly realizing that the divisions are merely a convenience we use to name our specialities; all the information discovered in any field is a piece of our ever-growing, ever-resolving model of the universe. It is this model that unites people; all races in all cultures can improve the model. We do so by observing its parts, then adding more, taking some off or improving the ones there, as we see fit. Certainly, then, the question "When will the model be finished?" comes to mind. When time can be described in any situation, when solution methods for partial differential equations are completely generalized in one theory, when a quantum theory of gravity is stumbled upon, when frictional forces like those that make a match flare are described on the atomic and subatomic level, in other words, not in the near future. I personally find this very reassuring; history demonstrates that we need never fear running out of problems to solve.

Leo Tolstoy once described history as analogous to calculus. To him, humanity ebbed and flowed in a series of events and actions that reminded him of a continuous function. Finding the motivations and causes was then, to him, like integrating a continuous function: the sum of "the differential of history, that is, the individual tendencies of men." I find in this a fascinating example for the behavior of us all: to solve the problems of tomorrow, we will have to connect areas of knowledge previously isolated from each other. It has already been happening for years; in the future the process will most likely accelerate. For example, imagine biology today without any input at all from higher mathematics, computer modeling, or theoretical chemistry. The progress made in biology in recent years requires knowledge developed in these fields and others. As it stands now, mathematicians can look forward both to answering questions in their own fields as well as providing input for problems in all other fields of knowledge. This, more than anything else, is what I want to do.

It now seems a simple and reasonable conclusion that the best career choice for me is in mathematics; this was not always so. It was in sixth grade, at age eleven, that I made the sudden and stunning realization that mathematics was not merely a long set of rules regarding addition, subtraction, multiplication, and division. My math teacher had started presenting peculiar math problems of the sort I had noticed before in my own everyday pursuits: problems that required one to work backwards inverting operations to discover an unknown. I was excited at the time because I could see that generalizing this type of problem into different, exact methods for finding the solutions was an extremely important task. From the school library I checked out a book called *The Realm of Algebra* by Isaac Asimov to find out more about this. The true enormity of mathematics struck me when Asimov described the evolution of the complex number system.

What did mathematicians do when they found that no real numbers can be squared to give a negative real numbers? Not acknowledging any former precepts, they simply invented more numbers. It seemed to me that they had to break rules to do this; I found out later that much scientific progress is made by breaking old rules and tossing out old ideas. Since I have always very much enjoyed questioning old ideas and breaking rules, I knew then that I would have to pursue this subject further. Mathematics now seems to me to be a peculiar mix of things invented and things discovered. Studying it and making progress in it requires both inspiration on a par with that required to write good poetry, and the strict adherence to logic which is necessary to persuade one's peers. All in all, I do not doubt the subject's capacity to intrigue me (and thousands of others) for centuries.

# ANALYSIS

Field's essay is an articulate exploration of the development of an academic interest in mathematics. The essay is particularly striking because the entire package shows that Field is well-rounded: a technical topic written in an engaging and literary style. The ideas presented in the essay are thought-provoking ways to think about mathematics. By analogizing mathematics to history and poetry, Field demonstrates a certain sophistication in that understanding mathematics in the larger sphere of human knowledge, rather than as a narrowly defined field. The essay also has a pleasant balance of the abstract and concrete personal experiences. While the prose in the middle of the essay is thought out and carefully crafted, both the introduction and ending have a bit of a "tacked on" feel. In addition, the transition to the last paragraph of how choosing his career is "a simple and reasonable conclusion" is also slightly awkward. The essay reads as though paragraphs were written independently and then sewn together at the end. Spend time on your introduction and conclusion as they are the first and last impression the reader receives.

—Jennifer 8. Lee

# "Thoughts Behind a Steam-Coated Door"

By Neha Mahajan, who attended a public high school in Boulder, Colorado.

*Till taught by pain Men really know not what good water's worth.*

—Lord Byron

A light gauze of steam coats the transparent door of my shower. The temperature knob is turned as far as it can go, and hot drops of water penetrate my skin like tiny bullets. The rhythm of water dancing on the floor creates a blanket of soothing sound that envelops me, muffling the chaotic noises of our thin-walled house. Tension in my back that I didn't even know existed oozes out of my pores into streams of water cascading in glistening paths down my body. I breathe in a mist of herbal scented shampoo and liquid Dove soap, a welcome change from the semi-arid air of Colorado. In the shower I am alone. No younger siblings barging unannounced into my room, no friends interrupting me with the shrill ring of the telephone, no parents nagging me about finishing college essays.

The ceramic tiles that line my bathroom wall have the perfect coefficient of absorption for repeated reflections of sound waves to create the wonderful reverberation that makes my shower an acoustic dream. The two by four stall is transformed into Carnegie Hall as Neha Mahajan, world-renowned musician, sings her heart out into a shampoo bottle microphone. I lose myself in the haunting melisma of an aalaap, the free singing of improvised melodies in classical Indian music. I perfect arrangements for a capella singing, practice choreography for Excalibur, and improvise songs that I will later strum on my guitar.

Sometimes I sit in the shower and cry, my salty tears mingling with the clear drops upon my face until I can no longer tell them apart. I have cried with the despair of my friend and mentor in the Rape Crisis Team when she lost her sister in a vicious case of domestic abuse, cried with the realization of the urgency of my work. I have cried with the inevitable tears after watching *Dead Poet's Society* for the seventh time. I have cried with the sheer frustration of my inability to convince a friend that my religious beliefs and viewpoints are as valid as hers. Within these glass walls I can cry, and my tears are washed away by the stinging hot water of the shower.

The water that falls from my gleaming brass showerhead is no ordinary tap water. It is infused with a mysterious power able to activate my neurons. My English teachers would be amazed if they ever discovered how many of my compositions originated in the bathroom. I have rarely had a case of writer's block that a long, hot shower couldn't cure. This daily ritual is a chance for me to let my mind go free, to catch and reflect over any thoughts that drift through my head before they vanish like the ephemeral flashes of fireflies. I stand with my eyes closed, water running through my dripping hair, and try to derive the full meaning conveyed in chapter six of my favorite book, *Zen and the Art of Motorcycle Maintenance*. I'll be lathering shampoo into the mass of tangles that is my hair as I work on a synaesthesia for the next two lines of a poem, or the conditioner will be slowly soaking through when I experience an Archimedean high, as a hard-to-grasp physics concept presented earlier in the day suddenly reveals itself to me. Now, if only they had let me take that AP Calculus test in the shower . . .

The sparkles of falling water mesmerize me into reflection. Thoughts tumbling in somersaults soften into a dewy mellowness. Do these drops of water carry a seed of consciousness within them? As I watch the water winking with the reflected light of the bathroom, it appears to glow in the fulfillment of its karma. Then, for a split second, all thoughts cease to exist and time stands still in a moment of perfect silence and calm like the mirror surface of a placid lake.

I know I have a tendency to deplete the house supply of hot water, much to the annoyance of the rest of my family. I know I should heed my mother's continual warnings of the disastrous state of my skin after years of these long showers; as it is, I go through two bottles of lotion a month to cure my post-shower "prune" syndrome. But my shower is too important to me. It is a small pocket of time away from the frantic deadline and countless places to be and things to do. It is a chance to reflect, and enjoy—a bit of welcome friction to slow down a hectic day. The water flows into a swirling spiral down the drain beneath my feet. It cleanses not only my body, but my mind and soul, leaving the bare essence that is me.

## ANALYSIS

This essay illustrates how something as ordinary as a hot shower can be used auspiciously to reveal anything of the author's choosing. Mahajan could have focused on the academic subjects or extracurriculars she mentions in her essay, such as physics or the Rape Crisis Team, but instead she chooses a daily ritual common to us all. Though everyone can relate to taking a shower, doubtless few shower in quite the same way Mahajan does or find it to be such an intellectually and emotionally stirring experience. The intimacy of the act sets an appropriate stage for her personal description of unraveling from life's stresses by singing into a shampoo bottle microphone.

There is no single, clear focus to the essay, but this accurately reflects the shower experience itself—"to catch and reflect over any thoughts that drift through my head before they vanish." Mahajan touches on schoolwork, classical Indian music, and contemplation about her favorite book, all with humorous flair, and she even goes into emotionally revealing descriptions of crying in the shower. Unfortunately, she dwells on crying for an entire paragraph, and the reader cannot help but wonder whether she could survive without her shower to cleanse her "mind and soul." Ultimately, that Mahajan derives literally so much inspiration and relief from the shower seems rather hard to believe. The notion that she could have done better on her AP Calculus test had she been allowed to take it in the shower is amusing, but doesn't seem to add much beyond the suggestion that she is dependent upon these showers. And that she finally did understand that vague "hard-to-grasp physics concept" seems excessive. Already she distinctly conveys her interest in science through her language—"the perfect coefficient of absorption for repeated reflections of sound waves"—and a supposedly subtle reaffirmation of this interest seems unnecessary.

Mahajan's vivid language and unusual descriptions are principle qualities of this essay. She deftly avoids the temptation of resorting to clichés, and most everything is entirely unpredictable. A relatively minor point is that her economy of language could be improved, as otherwise fluid sentences are occasionally overdone with an excess of adjectives and adverbs. Nonetheless, Mahajan conveys her talent for creative writing, and this carries her essay far beyond the lesser issues mentioned earlier. And, of course, her distinctive shower theme helps this exhibition of talent stand out.

—Ronald Y. Koo

# "Interview with Myself"

By Wesley Oliver, who attended a small public school in Jersey City, New Jersey.

The aroma of freshly brewed designer coffee saunters through the air and hugs the agreeable patrons of this Chelsea coffeehouse like a party hostess. She greets me. This visit to my favorite downtown Manhattan coffeehouse on this rainy Saturday afternoon is one of my few, rare opportunities to elude the pressures of work and middle age. Whenever I visit, I am sure to bring along my journal. Today, I decide instead to bring along one of my old journals from high school, to sift through pages of parties, broken hearts, and missed chances, and to mine them into some coherent impression of who I was, who he is. My mind wavers between thoughts of past and present.

Since those early school days of researching, calculating, and writing until sleep no longer divided the days, I have been researching, calculating, and writing for a living. Journalism is my love: meeting strangers, becoming inappropriately intimate with the affairs of their lives, then distributing that information for consumption by other strangers; few pleasures exceed that of seeing "By Wesley Oliver." But I have had other flirtations, particularly with the theater. Life has been generous, but demanding.

Feelings of nostalgia cause me to look back on my life and reach for those foggy, long-departed memories. And then he dashes in. Our conversation is unfettered by laws of time or the stubbornness of reality. Seventeen years old, he collapses his drenched umbrella and wipes his feet on the hazelnut-stained carpeting. "I love the rain," he half-chuckles to himself, emitting a smile that agrees, and one that will appear with just about everything he says. "It is an honor to meet you, sir," my then says to my now. "I have been watching you for years on your news program, and I saw you several years ago when you were an actor on Broadway. You are who I want to be." His eyes speak of admiration and envy.

"Well, my full name actually is Reginald Wesley Joseph Oliver," he says with restrained pride. He rattles on about how he's wanted to be a journalist since he was six, how English is his favorite subject, how New York is his favorite place, how he'd love to spend an afternoon with Sydney Carton to learn "selflessness and the gift of sacrifice," and how enthralled he is with NBC. "I've been watching it forever," he gushes, "and I cannot wait to be a journalist there. I guess it's my own little idiosyncrasy."

There is something about him. Something familiar yet estranged. Something that reintroduces me to idealism and the idea that the world is a malleable, dynamic place waiting not to be conquered, but fulfilled.

A passing salt-and-pepper nylon raincoat chafes my arm and rouses me from my reflection. Its owner and I share an awkward glance, she of apology and I of sorrow. Now vanished, that meeting of men and merging of minds crystallized our life. It became clear: that naïve kid grew up, learned something, and became someone. He is the poetry of my journal and my life, forever in me helping renavigate those choppy, uncertain waves long forgotten and soon recharted.

## ANALYSIS

Trumpeting one's accomplishments while remaining modest is a difficult task, but it is a challenge applicants will inevitably face in the personal essay. Mr. Oliver uses a creative conceit to walk this line between self-promotion and self-effacement, by imagining a meeting between his present and future selves. We gradually realize that the narrator is in fact adult Wesley, already an established journalist and once "an actor on Broadway." Mr. Oliver uses this technique to list his aspirations and career goals in an imaginative and dynamic way, avoiding the generic clunker of "This is what I want to be when I grow up." We're impressed by his technique and his chosen careers, journalism and drama, a refreshing change from the parade of would-be doctors, lawyers, and brokers that march through Ivy League admissions offices.

Mr. Oliver conveys the college application essentials—life goals, a few choice details about his interests, a hint at his academic path ("English is his favorite subject")—but the essay sets itself apart with its close attention to aesthetic detail. Mr. Oliver is not quite showing off, but he's close: every line is pregnant with stylistic flourishes and a journalist's eye for atmospheric detail ("aroma of freshly brewed designer coffee"). He sets the scene with highly descriptive language, placing the reader in a concrete and tactile setting ("This visit to my favorite downtown Manhattan coffeehouse on this rainy Saturday afternoon"). The writing is overdone at times, occasionally swinging from poetic to pretentious ("Now vanished, that meeting of men and merging of minds crystallized our life"). But Mr. Oliver more than establishes his highly developed literary talents and charts an ambitious course. His assertion that the world is a "dynamic place waiting not to be conquered, but fulfilled" leaves the reader with the sense that Mr. Oliver is determined to go places—and take an unconventional path.

—Michael M. Grynbaum

# "A Grateful Glance into Trash"

By David Soloveichik, who attended a small private high school in Los Angeles, California.

I spent hours staring at trash. Often, rather than going home, playing games outside with other four-year-olds, or watching cartoons, I insisted that my grandmother take me to the local rubbish dump. I was still in Kiev then, and piles of technological trash were quite common. There were remnants of bicycles, old television sets, broken cameras, pieces of mystical electronic equipment, cylinders, and other parts of internal combustion engines, all intriguing and exciting. A cylinder's head, still almost shiny, looked like a leg of a robot. What purpose did this metallic curiosity fulfill? Why was it made and then thrown into this pile of rusting, crumbling, variegated junk? This was a puzzle, a mechanical system with knowns and unknowns where I could always find a solution if I looked deeply enough. My mother warned me that if I kept wasting my time, I would grow up to be a garbageman. I told her that that's exactly what I wanted to become. She didn't understand that amid tires, cables, refrigerators, gyros, labels, and carburetors I found interest, imagination, and logical thought.

The garbage dump was the first arena of my intellectual upbringing. From then on my curiosity has always found something new, undiscovered, and fascinating. This curiosity leads me through life, from gears to automatic transmissions, from light bulbs to lasers. It guides me under strangers' cars and into construction zones. When my family and I immigrated to the U.S., it led me to stare, amazed, at automatic doors and supermarket scanners. However, the first time my curiosity was truly sparked was among those glistening metallic pieces of trash. Garbage trucks or lymphocytes, automatic doors or membrane channel proteins, cylinders or ATP pumps—from then on my world was always full of working little parts that could be understood, dissected, and logically analyzed.

I am now seventeen and pursuing my research, not at a garbage dump, but at the equipped laboratories of the high school, the computer at home, and this summer at the UCLA biotechnology laboratory. The logical connections I now make are between mathematical theorems, physical principles, and program functions. I dissect pieces of DNA using restriction enzymes and use light to analyze the chemical composition of stars. But I still like, from time to time, to take a grateful glance into trash: the evidence of society's creativity and ingenuity. One never knows what inspiration can be found there.

## ANALYSIS

With elegant understatement, this author turns a childhood fascination with garbage into a well-polished, sophisticated essay. Employing vivid description and concise prose, the author captures the raw emotion of a child's curiosity and uses it to highlight both his intellectual and individual growth. In doing so, his work proves that a successful essay need not tackle the meaning of life or challenge a widely held ideal in order to carry significant weight with a reader. Even within the bounds of the relatively brief three-paragraph piece, this author is able to detail a number of very personal experiences—his upbringing, immigration to the United States and intellectual awakening—all under the guise of garbage.

From the first sentence, the author is particularly successful at drawing the reader in and keeping his or her attention through the entire piece. The image of the author as child, staring at trash, creates an immediate sense of tension and forces the reader to ponder why this is in fact the case. But the writer does not let up, and uses direct questions to force the reader to stay an active participant in the narrative. By the same token, the opening sentence of the essay's middle paragraph provides an effective and intriguing transition that helps reinforce the essay's well-established sense of flow.

Despite the overall strength of the work, however, the author puts a slight damper on his piece with a less-than-impressive final sentence. Although in the second to last sentence the author skillfully brings the reader full circle to the essay's opening point, his conclusion loses steam. By simply removing the last sentence, the essay could end on a strong and elegant note.

—Scott A. Resnick

# "Catharsis in Uncluttering"

By Katherine Chan, who attended a small private school in Jamaica Estates, New York.

Narrowly escaping an unceremonious death by suffocation on the E train, I restlessly waddled up the Roosevelt Station steps to discover my beloved city in a mist of unprecedented chaos. It was enjoyably innovative, really. Realizing that flooded city buses would not magically empty as a personal favor to me, I skipped the merry three miles home all the while recalling the last scenes of *Atlas Shrugged*. Midway down Elmhurst Avenue passing the fourth distraught bodega owner I realized that refrigerators were not immune to blackouts, that despite the general omnipotence of the food-providing contraption, it too relied on electricity. With this unsettling thought as my sole motivation, I sprinted home in record-breaking time.

Sitting by a hemp candle later that night, I rescued my third tub of Edy's. It was only after my sixth wave of nausea that I finally abandoned my act of heroism, fell backwards, belly to the ceiling, unable to support my body weight. My older brother felt it was amusing and necessary to walk to my head, rest his foot on my face and say, "This would bite if we had to live like this." Annoyed but powerless to resist due to my overconsumption of fat, I retorted, "Actually, Pez, I kinda like this. Relaxing yet thought provoking." He grunted, removed his foot and left.

That night, as the rest of New York City was suffering from what is now notoriously known as the BLACKOUT OF 2003 I entertained the concept of simplicity—starting life on a deserted island (ELECTRICITY included) and loading only crucial possessions onto my dinghy as I set out for my island of Chicken and Broccoli.

**Yam Beans**—*"My daddy loves yams, because when he was young and had nothing to eat, yams were always there for him, and that's why*

*Daddy calls me his yam."* My father never spoke of the Revolution, never spoke of the nationalization of family lands, never spoke of siblings he would never see again. From his youth he only mentioned two things: grandma and yams. The mental image of my grandmother bending forward in a rice paddy with a baby, who was to be my father tied to her back, has forever been immortalized with the subtitle "if there's a will, there's a way." Yams kept my father alive when ration cards weren't enough, as they never were. Yams were his life source; he ate them to proclaim his right to live, and so I was lovingly called.

**Eternal subscription to the Sunday *New York Times***—Fifteen sections, a magazine, and the most distressing crossword puzzles the world has ever known. Reading the Sunday *Times* from cover to cover takes approximately a week, understanding everything I read takes another week. Devouring an average of two sections a day, I have digested duck preening skills, Schwarzenegger's Republican frenzy, and plenty in between. Granted the *Times* is not the be and end all, instead it serves to present a panorama of possible new loves. Where else could I find the urge to crusade about a five-letter word for "Ancient Greek Tongue: Var"? All this for only three dollars and fifty cents.

**Swimsuit**—Nothing is as mind clearing as physical exhaustion; nothing as enjoyable as defying gravity. Both are conveniently attainable in swimming. Forward is the only important notion when swimming. Forward. Forward. Forward. Harder. Longer. Stronger. During certain laps, two-thirds of the way down the lane, lactic acid builds up to a point where my muscles scream for a spontaneous combustion. These are the most desirable moments of the sport because once they're past, all enigmas unravel and I know nothing is out of my reach. Forget alternate nostril breathing.

Such thoughts of cold aromatically chlorine water aggravated the infernally humid conditions. Irritated, I ran to my brother and unnecessarily stepped on his face. He chased me onto the porch until I screamed for mercy. After establishing peace, we lethargically laid on the steps staring into the tangible night.

08.14.2003. Took the electrical death of five states before I could see stars in New York City. I wonder what Times Square looks like dark. Must be frighteningly beautiful.

## ANALYSIS

This essay's strongest feature is that the writer takes her experience of one event—the blackout in New York City in 2003—and describes it in such a way that it sheds light on several different sides of her personality. The reader learns from Chan's essay not only that she's a New Yorker who loves ice cream, but also that she has a passion for swimming, is proud of her ethnic heritage, and has a teasing relationship with her brother. Chan comes across as personable and friendly in the essay, and her genuine nature also shines through.

Chan also uses a large and descriptive set of vocabulary to describe her actions and mental states during her adventure. It is very much to her credit that she uses very few "to be" verbs, and more descriptive action verbs like "waddled," "sprinted," and "skipped." In a college essay, word choice is very important, because if it's too long or loquacious the reader will get bored and not truly glean what you have to say.

Chan's intellectual curiosity also shines through in this essay. She refers to the rather thick novel *Atlas Shrugged* in passing, and also mentions her love for the difficult *New York Times* Sunday crossword puzzle.

However, her topic is not particularly unique. Out of all the applicants from New York City, there must have been more than one on the blackout. If you're going to do a topic that other people would consider doing (for example, your thoughts on the presidential election), you might want to steer clear unless you have a very unique perspective on the topic (for example, you are a candidate's daughter).

The reader might also be a little disoriented at the format. After discussing her travels home during the blackout, Chan launches into a description of three things she'd want to have with her if she were on a desert island. It seems to be a non sequitur, and the reader might notice that the essay doesn't flow because of the pretty rapid change in format and topic without a clear transition. Chan switches from simple prose to a bullet-point type of format to a diary entry at the end. A reader could be a bit taken aback by the sudden shifts in style.

And while Chan's vocabulary is certainly impressive, there are times when she waxes a bit over-descriptive, to the point that phrases sound awkward. For example, the phrase "annoyed but powerless to resist due to my overconsumption of fat" could be a solid adjectival phrase if the number of words and their complexity was cut down. By trying to cram in so many expressive words, Chan is losing the flow of the piece and the reader can get bogged down in the words instead of caught up in the story. Another example of this wordiness is the phrase: "general omnipotence of the food-providing contraption," referring to a refrigerator. Don't use impressive words for the sake of using them; make sure you're using them in the right context.

—Hana R. Alberts

# SONGS OF EXPERIENCE

# "Should I Jump?"

By Timothy F. Sohn, who attended a medium-sized public high school in
Tarrytown, New York.

As I stood atop the old railroad-bridge some six stories above the
water, my mind was racing down convoluted paths of thought:
Logic and reason would oblige me to get off this rusting trestle, run to
my car, fasten my seat belt, and drive home carefully while obeying the
speed limit and stopping for any animals which might wander into my
path. This banal and utterly safe scenario did not sit well with me. I felt
the need to do something reckless and impetuous.

"Why am I doing this?"

I backed up to where I could no longer see the huge drop which
awaited me, and then, my whole body trembling with anticipation, I
ran up to the edge, and hurled myself off the bridge.

"Do I have a death wish? Will my next conversation be with Elvis or
Jimmy Hoffa?"

The first jump off the bridge was like nothing I had ever experienced. I do not have a fascination with death, and I do not display sui-
cidal tendencies, yet I loved throwing myself off that bridge, despite
the objections of the logical part of my brain. Standing up there, I recalled from physics that I would be pulled toward the earth with an ac-
celeration of 9.8m/s/s. G-forces meant nothing to me once I stepped off
the edge of the bridge, though. I felt like I was in the air for an eternity
(although I was actually only in the air for about three seconds).

This leap was at once the most frightening and most exhilarating experience of my life. That synergy of fear and excitement brought about
a unique kind of euphoria. Jumping off and feeling the ground fall out
from underneath me was incredible. I have rock-climbed and rap-
pelled extensively, but those experiences cannot compare, either in
fear or in thrill, to jumping off a bridge.

Once I conquered my initial fear and jumped off, I did it again and again, always searching for that tingling sensation which ran through my limbs the first time I did it, but never quite recapturing the astonishing bliss of that first jump. I have jumped many times since that first time, and all of my jumps have been fun, but none can quite match that first leap. The thrill of that first jump, that elusive rapture, was one of the greatest feelings of my life.

"Wow, I can't believe I did that!"

When I jumped off that bridge, I was having fun, but I was also rebelling. I was making amends for every time I did the logical thing instead of the fun thing, every time I opted for the least dangerous route throughout my life. I was rising up and doing something blissfully bad, something impetuous. I was acting without thinking of the ramifications, and it was liberating. My whole life, it seemed, had been lived within the constrictive boundaries of logical thought. I overstepped those boundaries when I jumped. I freed myself from the bonds of logic and reason, if for only a few seconds, and that was important.

## ANALYSIS

In this essay, Sohn presents a captivating narrative of an experience that has significantly shaped his attitudes and outlook on life. In order for this narrative form to be successful, the writer must use descriptive language to set the scene and transport the reader to the location and even into the thought process of the narrator. Sohn does this remarkably well. The reader can envision the railroad trestle upon which he stands and even feel the weightlessness of his free-fall thanks to clear, descriptive language. Sohn uses a mature vocabulary and incorporates an internal dialogue to aid the flow of his essay successfully.

The inevitable goal of such a format is for the writer to convey something about his or her personality or individual qualities to the reader. In this case, Sohn wanted the reader to know about his freewheeling side; his ability to take risks, defy logic, and experience danger. The conclusion is also a particular strength of this essay. Sohn takes the isolated event he has described so well and applies it to a broader scheme, showing the reader just how this event was truly significant to his life.

—Adam S. Cohen

# "Grandma's Living Room"

By Rosa Norton, who attended a medium-sized public high school in San Antonio, Texas.

I settled back into the familiar couch in my grandparents' living room, a room I had known all my life. My gaze flickered over the cold, hard, tiled floor I used to sleep on with my cousins, up to the cross on the wall, and finally came to rest on the fat lady dishware on the dining room table where my mother sat, plates that my five aunts had collected for Grandma. I looked back at my mom, wondering what she was thinking about. She had known this setting most of her life, too, and she kept coming back.

"Mama, I have homework. I spent half the day yesterday at Aunt Sylvia's birthday party, and then I woke up early because you insisted on going to 10:30 mass. I want to go home," I had said as we left church.

Silent for a time, my mother kept her eyes forward as she drove. I closed mine, listening to the classical music wafting through the car. When we first moved back to San Antonio, she had driven around with her windows down, blaring Tejano music from her stereos, something she had never done up North. In recent years she had stopped the habit, perhaps because it embarrassed my sister and me. She still wore bright colors, though. In church, my grays and blues would rest on her pinks and reds.

"Your grandparents miss you, honey."

"All right, I'll go," I sighed, releasing the guilt bottled inside me.

Now the frying pan sizzled from the kitchen as my grandparents cooked chorizo and corn tortillas, Grandma in her house dress and Grandpa in his white shirt, soiled from gardening. Next to them, my great-grandfather watched proudly, leaning on a restaurant counter from his black-and-white perch on the wall. He had owned his own restaurant. Chorizo for fifteen cents.

"Poor Julie," Grandma said, leaning her head back to talk to us from the kitchen. "Jesse says she hasn't stopped crying."

Julie and I had played with Barbies together as girls. We were distant relatives, but I had just thought of her as a friend. We had sat on the floor in Grandma's middle room, one blond-haired girl from Massachusetts and one black-haired girl from the poor side of San Antonio, giggling shyly over our dolls. We lost touch with each other before either of us entered middle school.

Julie had had a baby when she was sixteen. My mother had delivered her. Now, Julie's ex-boyfriend's mother had taken the baby from her, claiming she was unfit to be a parent. Julie was distraught.

As I listened, I began thinking of ways to help Julie, whose family had deserted her at a young age, leaving her with my great uncle. I finally stopped. Would Julie really want my help?

I looked at my mother again. Her head was bowed; she looked tired, sad, but not shocked. After all, she dealt with cases like this all the time, working on the poor side of San Antonio as an obstetrician. She had grown up in this house, poor, and worked her way through medical school in order to have the freedom to leave. But she always came back.

The life I was born into had been different from hers. My father, an Anglo man from Washington State, and she had raised me in Massachusetts. They named me Rosa—Rosa, after Grandma Rosa and the saint, from my mother, and Rosa, after Rosa Parks and Rosa Luxemburg, from my father. The dichotomy never confused me; I was simply Rosa, the loved one.

Now we had moved back to San Antonio, our family of four, with its strong, separate identity. We lived in the same city, but in different neighborhoods, different worlds. I had often wondered why Mama was so adamant about regular visits to my grandparents. Now, as I sat and listened to them talk about Julie, who had never had the large family my mother grew up with, I understood. Family, despite all its complications, meant love. And in this world, the more love, the better.

# ANALYSIS

Writing an essay about family members may be difficult. However, writing about the effects of socioeconomic stratification is often harder—the topic is extremely delicate, and unless one has lived through an experience first-hand, discussion of this issue should generally be avoided. What makes this essay memorable, then, is Norton's ability to combine both elements of family and socioeconomic reality into a compelling tale of what family means to her.

Norton achieves this synthesis through her descriptive characterization and well-chosen narrative structure. Reading phrases like "blasting Tejano music from her stereos" and "chorizo for fifteen cents," we realize that Norton's family is deeply cultural, independent, and resourceful. Furthermore, her narrative of Julie is poignant without being overly dramatic. While Norton acknowledges the contrasting lives that she and Julie live, she refrains from being patronizing by considering the other side: "Would Julie want my help?" This careful crafting of Julie's world, combined with the colorful descriptions of her own family, portrays Norton as a thoughtful, mature applicant who appreciates intergenerational ties and her family's love.

While the essay is strong overall, its introduction has room for improvement. Although the first paragraph establishes the setting for the rest of the essay, its effect is rather diminished by unwieldy syntax. Also, the essay might be strengthened by moving some of the characterization of Norton's mother in the third paragraph further down in the essay. While the background information is interesting, it detracts from the flow of the mother-daughter conversation, which is vital to the piece. Finally, the last sentence is overly broad and lacks a personal voice. The essay would end more perfectly without it.

—Risheng Xu

# "A Mountain School Perspective"

Anonymous

Running late, I sprint out the door of Conard Dorm onto the slick, icy road on a Sunday morning so cold that the thermometers have stopped reading. Thoughts of impending calculus projects, poems by Robert Frost idealizing such mornings, and more importantly the impatient bleats of unfed, pregnant sheep and an equally unhappy and entirely prosaic farm manager buzz through my head. I run faster. I wonder what I would be doing if I were at home now—probably sleeping. A year ago I never would have cloistered myself in the Green Mountains with forty-four farmer-students for a semester. And yet there I was living at The Mountain School of Milton Academy, a semester-long combination of academic and agricultural education.

Anyone who knew me before applying would never have thought that I would leave high school to attend a program I knew practically nothing about. I resisted changing my toothpaste much less my living space for four months. I acquired such a comfortable niche and stable group of friends (as opposed to a stable of sheep) throughout my years at Hopkins that I wanted to remain. But then something within me contradicted this advice—how much I would regret this unique chance to explore—and my friends echoed this theme.

I finally left my little cookie-cutter suburb of Hamden for the smaller and infinitely more remote town of Vershire, Vermont. On the first day, my anxiety about my roommate seemed fully justified by Raf: tight, paint-stained, black jeans, a blue, punk-rock jacket with iron studs around the collar, and a mohawk haircut complete with a rat tail. My jaw dropped. But Raf rapidly broke every stereotype and became my closest friend, in the process teaching me lessons in tolerance and shattering my naiveté.

Food provoked another source of shock—and expansion. I had always and heedlessly eaten whatever my mother put on the table, until I learned more about the origins of the food I ate. Weekly farm seminars educated me about the pros and cons of organic and genetically modified foods. My food investigation culminated in an elective visit to a slaughterhouse to see the intermediate step between the cattle fields and the hamburger. That visit opened my eyes to the true story of every red-meat product I had ever eaten. To this day I can vividly remember the image of the massive heifer hitting the ground. I decided to continue to eat red meat in smaller quantities, but only after a week of vegetarianism and contemplation.

Every Mountain School student's experience includes a four-day solo in the woods, a daunting and even frightening prospect for an urbanite for whom "nature" meant a manicured lawn, and "alone" meant an evening at home. Nevertheless, I survived. Solo provided a time for introspection and exploration in the literal sense. I spent those days writing in my journal, tracking moose, and making up juvenile games to interest myself. I would never have thought to spend time without sensory bombardment in solitude without attending The Mountain School.

So although I no longer feed lambing sheep every morning and my daily routine no longer involves herding cows, I do still keep the tolerance and respect learned at The Mountain School in my heart. Back at Hopkins, I rush from class to class, not dorm to barn, glad that I took a risk and did not fail—that I finally broke out of my niche.

## ANALYSIS

The writer begins this essay with a clear and effective introduction, which concisely illustrates the contrast between The Mountain School and his normal life, and indicates the thesis of the piece.

The theme of an average "cookie-cutter" student going to the wilderness and learning to be a better person is a bit hackneyed, but the vivid anecdotes the writer uses to prove his point are detailed and vivid enough to compensate. Starting the essay with a present-tense portrayal of his morning run is exciting and draws the reader into the action. But the whirlwind of different scenes and anecdotes packed into a single-page document weakens the essay.

In an extremely concise piece such as those necessary for college applications, often, one focused, illustrative, and emblematic story is much stronger than a number of less-developed mentions of different activities. One of the sketches mentioned in this piece describes the writer's initial apprehension about his roommate evolving into respect and friendship. Another discusses his decision to change his eating habits, and still another, his "solo" experience. Any one of these could be a quite compelling support for his argument about the effects of his Mountain School experience on his identity, and an opportunity for him to show his descriptive and narrative skill. Juxtaposed in quick succession, however, they are confused and weakened. The few sentences allotted for each story allow barely more than an extremely cursory sketch, and while the writer does a fairly good job maximizing these few phrases, he cannot possibly explain the nuances and effects in a satisfactory manner. Delving into how Raf cut through the writer's stereotypes and naïveté, for example, would have been much more effective than simply stating that he did.

In touching on a number of fascinating anecdotes throughout the essay, the writer leaves us wondering about the details of each one. He should have followed a single story through its course, and then described its lasting effects on his life after The Mountain School. Nevertheless, the writer's ability to take risks and learn from new experiences comes through strongly in his essay, which is full of vivid details and moments of personal growth.

—Katherine A. Kaplan

# "One Hundred Pairs of Eyes"

By Patricia M. Glynn, who attended a rural public high school in
Plymouth, Massachusetts.

Awareness. An awareness that all eyes from one hundred yards of
green grass are focused on a certain point in space is what drives
through my thoughts as I stand poised. These eyes disregard the pe-
ripheral chatter of spectators, the cold wind whistling in the night air
around them, and the harshness of the white lights over the field. They
focus only on this one spot before my hands and, to begin their show,
they wait for a simple motion, a mere flick of the wrist. As a tingling
sensation arises in my fingertips, I lift my hands in preparation. One
hundred pairs of eyes breathe in unison across the hundred yards, and
my hands descend in a practiced pattern toward that one point in
space. It is that point where the hundred pairs of eyes release their
breath into their various instruments, where the music is created, and
where the show begins.

This experience is one that I get to relive every Friday night while
conducting the Plymouth High School marching band in its weekly
half-time performance for the football fans. While I have performed as
one of the pairs of eyes, as conductor and Senior Drum major I feel a
greater part of the show than I ever did before. I feel every note and
every phrase of music from every instrument, and I pull even more music from those instruments. Their intensity is sparked from my intensity, and mine builds on theirs. The intensity is not only from the
music; it comes from the eyes. It's my eyes scanning the field, scouting
for problems, and brokering confidence that command an intensity in
response. This is the greatest feeling in the world.

As my motions become larger and larger and my left hand pushes
upward, I demand volume from the band while it crescendos toward its
final notes. Building volume and drive, this music sends a tingling sen-

sation from my fingertips through my wrists and pulsing through my body. My shoulders ache but keep driving the beat, and my emotions are keyed up. As the brass builds and the band snaps to attention in the last picture of the show, the percussion line pushes the music with a driving hit. Musicians and conductor alike climax with the music until reaching that same instant in time. With a rigorous closing of my fists, the music stops, but the eyes hold their focus, instruments poised, until a smile stretches across my face and my features relax, tingling with pent up emotion. Applause.

## ANALYSIS

An essay that asks for discussion of an important extracurricular activity may be just the place for an applicant to discuss in greater detail why participating in student government makes his or her world go 'round. But as in this case, the essay may also offer an opportunity for an applicant to further describe a unique or unconventional interest. "One Hundred Pairs of Eyes" details the author's experiences as conductor of her high school football band—a position that on paper may not carry much weight, despite its many responsibilities. Through her description of leading one hundred musicians in the complexities of a half-time show, the reader gains unique insight into being at the helm of a marching band—a position from which few people have observed the perspective.

The author begins her essays with rich description—she is the point of focus for one hundred sets of eyes. By personifying the eyes, the author paints a marvelous picture of the scene. The reader can almost sense the position from which she must be standing and the enormity of the group at her feet. But he or she is left to wonder what sort of awkward situation may be causing this unique scenario. Just as the author creates an intense sensation of tension in the essay, the reader too holds his or her breath in advance of the announcement that Glynn is the leader of a marching band.

As she continues, the author contrasts her experiences as conductor with those of being a performer, shedding light on the exhilaration of holding the gaze of the hundred musicians who look to her for rhythm and tempo. And with descriptive language in the third paragraph, the author encourages the reader to push onward, toward the finale of both the music and the essay. The passage ends with an impressive sense of relief both for the band members and the reader.

—Scott A. Resnick

# "The Lost Game"

By Stephanie A. Stuart, who attended a small college-preparatory high school in Monterey, California.

When I was little my father used to play a game with me driving home. Its main substance was something like this: he would say, oh no, I seem to be lost; how shall we get home? And then he would ask, which way? Gleefully, I would crane my neck above the seat; according to the game, his befuddlement was hopeless, and I alone as navigator could bring us home. No doubt I seemed contrary as I directed him further and further down back streets, but my secret incentive was exploration. As a small child there is very little one can control in one's world; to have control over an entire grown-up—not to mention a whole car—was tremendously appealing. The real allure, though, was in going the "wrong" way—as soon as we turned left where we usually turned right, the world was so brand new it might have only appeared the moment we rounded the corner. My heart would beat below my throat as I gave the direction to turn, stretching my neck from my place in the backseat, eager and afraid: Suppose I did really get us lost? The secret desire to discover always won out over the fear, but I can still recall the flutter of my heart on the inside of my ribs as I navigated the roundabout connections which was as mysterious as the Northwest Passage, lone link between the cul-de-sacs.

Exploration was a quest I took to heart; alone, I would set out on expeditions into our back yard, or down the street, creating a mental map concentric to our doorstep. Discovery bloomed magical for me; marked on the map were the locations of abandoned tree houses, bell-blue flowers and plants with flat powdery leaves the size of silver dollars.

The other night it fell to my brother and me to return a movie. After we left it on the counter, though, our sense of adventure got the better of us. Oh dear, I said, I seemed to be lost. Where shall I go? Eager to discover the town which smoldered at one o'clock under the orange and violet of sodium street lamps, he chose the road less traveled, at least by our wheels.

We wound into the pine forest in the dead of night; moonlight feel eerie across our laps, striated by tree trunks. I crested a hill slowly: Monterey spread in a lighted grid below us, down to the darkening sea.

Above, the Milky Way sprang apart and arched like a dance. I angled my ear for a moment to Gatsby's tuning fork, that pure, enticing tone that echoes from the spheres. Think, remember, I wished upon him, what it is to explore, and the explorer's incentive: discovery.

"Which way?" I asked him, and he grinned slowly, moonlight glinting far-off mischief in his eyes. The streets spread orthogonal before us; the pure realm of possibility opened from them.

"Straight ahead," he said, and I smiled.

## ANALYSIS

Stephanie's essay falls into the life experiences category. However, rather than focusing on a single life-changing experience, Stephanie shows her approach toward personal discovery by relating the story of riding in a car and changing the standard directions as a means of stumbling upon unexplored worlds. The essay is well controlled—at no point does she stray toward overstating the significance of these individual events, but deftly uses them as a tool to illustrate her adventure-seeking attitude toward life and her unwillingness to be satisfied with the routine. Stephanie further highlighted the importance of discovery when she submitted the essay to the admissions office on U.S. Geological Survey maps—a thoughtful touch.

The essay's greatest asset is the sense of personal development Stephanie conveys. What begins as a cute story of her childhood is used wonderfully to highlight her personal development as she writes of a tenet in her life: "Think, remember . . . what it is to explore, and the explorer's incentive: discovery." Stephanie avoids listing her accomplishments in a résumé put into sentence form, but still captures important aspects of her identity, namely her inquisitiveness. The essay is well-paced and calm, with a solid development from beginning to end. Stephanie describes sensory aspects of her story ("flat, powdery leaves the size of silver dollars") with great word choice without overdoing it. It is clear that every word in the essay was carefully chosen to accurately and succinctly describe her subject. Not only does her essay successfully paint a picture of her as a curious little child, it shows that the same inquisitiveness she exhibited then she still possesses, now coupled with more responsibility, as she drives her brother and encourages his inquisitiveness.

The biggest risk in this essay is that it does not adequately showcase her accomplishments, normally a standard part of a college essay. While it worked for her, this has much to do with the extraordinary level of care she took in crafting the essay; her diligence shows, and the essay is an insightful, well-written, and well-paced piece of work.

—Jason M. Goins

# "Warm Hearts and a Cold Gun"

By James A. Colbert, who attended a medium-sized private boarding school in Deerfield, Massachusetts.

I f a six-foot-tall man slinging a semi-automatic rifle had approached me in Greenfield, I probably would have screamed for help. However, being in a foreign land, unable even to speak the native tongue, my options of recourse were significantly limited. The looming creature, dressed mostly in black, with short, dark hair, proceeded to grasp my right hand. As a smile furtively crept across his face, he mouthed, "Time to get on the bus."

"What?" I nervously spurted at the cold weapon before me.

"I'm sorry. I didn't introduce myself," he said. "I'm Ofir, your counselor."

Completely unnerved, I hurried onto the bus to be sure the gun remained at his side. "Did you know one of our leaders is a guy with a gun?" I asked a girl from Philadelphia, sitting beside me.

"What did you expect? This is Israel, not New England."

At the end of my junior year I decided to go to Israel to escape from the stimulating but confining atmosphere of Deerfield Academy. I yearned for a new environment where I could meet students unlike the ones I knew, where I could explore a foreign culture, and where I could learn more about my religion. The brochure from the Nesiya Institute had mentioned a "creative journey" featuring hikes in the desert, workshops with prominent Israeli artists, dialogues between Arabs and Jews, and discussions on Israeli culture and Judaism, but nowhere had it mentioned counselors with rifles. I suddenly wondered if I had made the right decision.

Weeks later, sitting outside the Bayit Va'gan Youth Hostel as the sun began to sink in the Israeli sky, I smiled with reassurance. As I looked up from writing in my journal, a group of misty clouds converged to form an opaque mass. But the inexorable sun demonstrated her tenacity. One by one, golden arrows pierced the celestial canopy to illuminate the lush, green valley between Yad Vashem and the hills of western Jerusalem. I could feel holiness in those rays of golden light that radiated from the sun like spokes of a heavenly wheel.

That moment was one of the most spiritual of my life. The natural grandeur of the sight seemed to bring together the most meaningful experiences of my five weeks in Israel: watching the sunrise over the Red Sea, wading chest-deep through a stream in the Golan Heights, looking up at the myriad stars in the desert sky, exploring a cave in Negev, and climbing the limestone precipice of Masada. These natural temples far surpassed any limestone sanctuary built by man.

Shifting my gaze downwards, I noticed Ofir standing beside me with his eyes fixed on the sacred valley. At age twenty-five, his head was already balding, but the expression on his face, with his eyes stretched wide and his jaws parted, reminded me of a child starting with delight at a fish in an aquarium. For over a minute neither of us spoke. That poignant silence said more than a thousand words could ever express.

Being an empirical person, I need confirmation, to prove to myself that I understood.

Finally, I said to Ofir, "This is holiness." His weapon bounced as he swiveled to look me in the eye. As he nodded in affirmation, a beam of light transcended his pupils to produce a telling spark of corroboration.

Emerson said in "Nature," "The sun illuminates only the eye of man, but shines into the eye and heart of the child." I carried an L. L. Bean backpack, and Ofir carried an Uzi, but that afternoon as the sun warmed our hearts, we were both children.

## ANALYSIS

The topic of this essay works well because it conveys the author's personal growth from a unique experience. His declaration of his decision to leave the atmosphere of his boarding school to travel abroad establishes him as a student willing to broaden his horizons and venture to the unknown. The initial comparison of Israel to his hometown is thoughtfully phrased and expresses his honest feelings.

The author is extremely concise in this essay, describing everything that is necessary and leaving out unnecessary details. His personal voice is evident. Rather than give plain descriptions of the places he visited, the author recalls his personal reaction to seeing such places, therefore allowing the reader to get to know the writer's own perspective.

The dialogue in this essay is also succinct, but complete. The author integrates other voices in his essay because those voices are part of his experience abroad. Finally, the closing quote from Emerson's "Nature" is well used and ties together with the poignant imagery of the contrasting L. L. Bean backpack and Uzi, leaving the reader with a vision of what the writer experienced.

—Nancy Poon

# "In the Waiting Room"

By Carlin E. Wing, who attended a small private high school in Brooklyn, New York.

You will not think, my mind firmly informed me; you are much too busy being nervous to think. I sat in the mother of all waiting rooms. My pen traveled frantically across the pages of my black book, recording every detail of the room in fragments that passed for poetry. I tried to write something deeply insightful about the procedure I was about to undergo but failed to produce even an opening sentence. These were the final minutes before my hand would be separated from my pen for ten weeks. Even if I could not think, I needed to write. My eyes became my pen and I wrote:

*Waiting Room*
    *the name dictates the atmosphere*
*The walls, papered in printed beige,*
    *are dotted with pastel pictures.*
*Two square columns interrupt the room,*
    *attended by brown plastic trash bins.*
*An undecided carpet of green, black, gray, red, blue*
    *mirrors the undecided feelings of the occupants.*
*And none of these mask the inevitable tension of the space.*

I paused and lifted my head to stare at The Door that led to my fate.

My fate was to have wrist surgery. Three years before, I had been told that the fracture in my wrist would heal. Earlier this year, I was again sitting in front of X-rays and MRI results listening to the doctor say that the old fracture had been an indication that the ligaments and tendons were torn. I could have declined to have surgery and never played competitive squash again. It was never an option.

I am a jock. My competitive personality finds a safe place to release itself on a playing field. My strongest motivation is the prospect of doing what no one expects I can do. However, the hardest competition I face is that of my own expectations. Squash allows me to put the perfectionist in me to good use. The beauty of squash, and sports in general, is that I never reach an anti-climax because there is always a higher level to reach for. Squash requires a healthy wrist. Surgery would make my wrist healthy. My immediate reaction to the doctor's words was "Yes, I want surgery. How soon can it be done? How long until I can play squash again? Can I watch?"

No one understood that last part. My parents jokingly told their friends about my desire to observe the surgery, and the doctor was adamantly opposed to the idea. But I had not been joking. It was my wrist they were going to be working on. I thought that entitled me to watch. Anyhow, I had never seen an operation and was fascinated by the idea of someone being able to sew a tendon back together. I had this image of a doctor pulling out the needle and thread and setting to work, whistling. Perhaps subconsciously I wanted to supervise the operation, to make sure that all the little pieces were sewn back into the right places (admittedly not a very rational thought since I wouldn't know by sight if they were sewing them together or tearing them apart). I understood the doctor's fear that I would panic and mess up the operation. Still, I wanted to watch. I felt it would give me a degree of control over this injury that had come to dominate my life without permission. Unfortunately, the final decision was not mine to make and the surgery was to go unrecorded by my eyes, lost in the memories of doctors who perform these operations daily.

The Door opened and I looked up, tingling with hope and apprehension. In response to the nurse's call a fragile elderly lady in a cashmere sweater and flowered scarf was wheeled towards The Door by her son. As she passed me I overheard her say, "Let's rock and roll." The words echoed in my ears and penetrated my heart. As I watched her disappear beyond The Door, I silently thanked her for the sudden dose of courage she had unknowingly injected in me. If she could do it, I could do it. I was next and before too long I was lying on a gurney in a room filled with doctors. I told the anesthesiologist that I did not want to be put to sleep, even though a curtain hid the actual operation from my sight. I said "Hi" to Dr. Melone and, as the operation began, sang contentedly along with The Blues Brothers.

## ANALYSIS

Chronicling an intimate moment or other personal experience requires particular attention and care in the essay-writing process. An author must be conscious that he or she creates an appropriate sense of balance that at once captures the reader while allowing for a sense of genuine personal reflection to show through. To be sure, the risk of turning the reader off with overly personal details or unnecessarily deep conclusions is a constant threat. However, "In the Waiting Room" reflects a successful attempt at convincing the reader that the author's wrist surgery merits his or her attention. Although unfocused, this work demonstrates that an essay about an otherwise insignificant topic can in fact be insightful and even touching.

By establishing a strong sense of tension at the beginning of the essay, "In the Waiting Room" succeeds where other personal reflection works often falter. The author does not begin with a topic sentence or other device that states the essay's point right away. To do so in this sort of essay would be to make the piece too much like a "what-I-did-last-summer" narrative. Instead, the reader is kept in suspense until the second paragraph of the piece of that which is causing the author's angst. Only then does the author spell out that it is his impending wrist surgery—and not a shot or test results—which has caused such great anxiety. As the essay continues, the author uses the occasion of waiting for the surgery to reflect on many of his complementary attributes: writer, athlete, coward and stoic. Overall, the writing is clear and unpretentious.

Yet in illustrating his multiple roles, the author tends to lose focus of the essay's overall point. Where it seems like the author portrays himself as an avid writer from the flow of the first paragraph, the reader is surprised to learn that the author is actually a self-described "jock" who plays squash. Before returning to the topic of the operation, the author takes another moment to reflect on his motivation for participating in sports. The essay loses significant steam and regains it only with the announcement that the author hopes to observe his own surgery. While interesting independently, these complications distract from the overall point. An essayist must be aware of the need to ensure that the flow of writing maintains a definite sense of direction—and doesn't meander too far from that path.

—Scott A. Resnick

# "My Responsibility"

By David J. Bright, who attended a large public high school in New York City.

When she hung up the phone, she immediately burst into tears and grabbed out in all directions for something to hold onto as she sank to the floor. I stood there motionless, not knowing what to do, not knowing what to say, not even knowing what had happened. It wasn't until I answered the door moments later and saw the police officers standing in the alcove that I finally discovered what had taken place. My fifteen-year-old brother had been arrested. It was only ten days before Christmas, a year ago today when it happened, but still I remember it like yesterday.

Robert had always been a rambunctious as a child—wild and lively, as my mom always said. He was constantly joking around, playing pranks, and causing mayhem, but his engaging personality and small stature always seemed to save him from the firing line. This gave him the notion that he could cause any amount of trouble without feeling the repercussions. As a youngster growing up in Ireland, he had found few opportunities to get into a great deal of trouble. But four years ago at the age of twelve, the rules changed for him when he, my mother and I moved to America.

The same short stature that had been his ally in Ireland was now Robert's enemy in America. He was bullied and beaten on a daily basis. Since I couldn't be there all the time, Robert sought the protection from others. By the end of his first year in America, he had already joined a gang.

His appearance deteriorated, personality disappeared, and aggressiveness increased, leaving him an angry, hollowed out, manic depressive. After a year or so, his frighteningly self-destructive behavior and terrifying appearance forced my mom to send him to a suicide treatment center. There he received round the clock attention, counseling, and medication for his depression and aggressiveness. He was released after a couple of months.

Only a few short weeks later, supposedly after mixing his medication with alcohol, he went out with his friends to go to the store. There they robbed, shot, and killed a store clerk. Robert, as an accomplice to the crime, was charged with armed robbery and second degree murder.

Looking back now, I realize not what Robert had done wrong, but what I had done wrong. I had taken no interest in his welfare, and I never intervened when he needed me to. I just sat back and let it all come crashing down around me. It's in this respect that I guess I've changed the most. I'm now a much more involved person. I no longer allow things to just happen; I must be a part of everything that affects me. I'm also a more caring and better person. To make up for what I did—or rather, didn't do—I look out for those around me, my family and my friends. I act like a big brother to them to compensate for not being any kind of brother at all to Robert.

The experience hasn't only made me better. In a strange way, it was also the best thing that could have happened to Robert. He's turned his life around and is presently preparing to take the SATs in anticipation to go on to college, something the old Robert would never have done.

I guess it's sort of weird, isn't it. Such a dreadful experience can change an entire family's life, and how such a tragic situation could give birth to such great things.

## ANALYSIS

Bright's intensely personal essay shows us the positive outcome of what seems like an overwhelmingly negative experience, that is, the arrest of his brother. Through his talkative, intimate writing style, Bright is able to reach his readers because he does not take a sentimental or moralistic tone. The strength of this essay lies in its honesty and its ability not only to criticize his brother, Robert, for his transgression, but to reprimand the author for his, as well. What makes this essay so unique is that Bright finds himself at fault and demonstrates his personal growth from his mistakes, unlike most college essays that are highly self-adulating in nature. Through accurately assessing where he went wrong by not acting like a true brother to Robert, Bright's piece is more impressive than most college essays.

Another great strength of Bright's essay is the maturity he displays by being able to take the blame for his brother's demise. This is a characteristic of a true big brother, one who knows how much his siblings admire and respect him, as well as value his judgment. Instead of harshly reproaching Robert for his crime, Bright turns to himself and how he "had taken no interest in his [Robert's] welfare." Furthermore, Bright illustrates how he was mature enough to learn from his errors and improve himself: "I act like a big brother . . . to compensate for not being any kind of brother at all to Robert." Bright is able to see that there are positive aspects of this bad experience and then applies them to his life; he shows to us that he is willing to change himself and make up for what he did not do for Robert by becoming "a much more involved person." In his essay, many aspects of Bright shine through: his maturity and strength, as well as his capacity to see a bright silver lining on what looks like a black thundercloud. Qualities such as these are ultimately the most important in terms of measuring who one is.

The only thing that Bright might have added to his essay is more of what happened to Robert. We learn that Robert was arrested, and is now studying for his SATs and preparing to go to college, but we are not told what happened to him between his arrest and his self-improvement. How did Robert decide to turn his life around? What challenges did he face? The second to last paragraph might need a little more detail as to how Robert went through the process of becoming who he is today. Yet, aside from this one minor comment, the essay stands on its own—it jumps out at the reader for its uniqueness, for its quiet, yet powerful, personal revelations.

—Marcelline Block

# "Lessons"

By G. Tyler O'Brien, who attended a large public school in Manchester, New Hampshire.

The first few weeks our conversations generically consisted of "Hey! How are you? That's great! OK day at school? Awesome. Up for some Ping Pong?" Recently, though, I had been making an effort to break through his tough exterior. After all, it was my job. I had joined the *Staying Cool After School* program at the Boys' and Girls' Club earlier that fall. I had joined with the intention of "making a difference." I was supposed to "reach" my mentee somehow. I was supposed to do in a few weeks what parents, siblings, guidance counselors and teachers hadn't been able to do in years.

"How about homework?" I asked.

"Ain't got any."

"Ain't got any? Wonderful. You have the rest of the night to show me where it says 'ain't' in the dictionary."

"I don't have any homework," he replied in a polite, strained tone.

Five minutes later we were sitting in the little library upstairs, staring at an open seventh-grade math book. Long division was not how I had envisioned ending my day. But that was my job, and I wanted to teach him, to help him. If a lesson in long division was what it took, so be it.

After four problems he did one on his own. My teaching methods had struck a nerve. Finally, a breakthrough. Before long, not only was he systematically working through each problem, but we were talking, and laughing. When he smiled, I smiled. We were getting somewhere. But it was 7:30, time to end the lessons for the evening. I walked him downstairs to meet his mom and say good night.

As we got to the door, a pair of headlights swung into the lot. The way they flashed across the small entrance area indicated their speed.

As the car got closer, it was clearly out of control. It attempted to pull into the first space, missing the lines completely. "There she is," Nate whispered. I said good night.

I hadn't reached the stairs before I heard the patter of footsteps behind me. "She's drunk." I didn't say anything. Nothing seemed to fit. I put my hand on his shoulder, and together we walked silently upstairs in search of the program's director. We called the police.

I stood alone in the empty parking lot and waved good-bye to the silhouette of my mentee in the back seat of a cruiser. I had joined the program expecting to teach life lessons to a misled kid who didn't have a grasp on what the real world was all about. I climbed into my mom's silver station wagon as the Crown Victoria with a cracking radio and flashing lights whirred into traffic.

As the police officer was opening the door to Nate's dark third-floor apartment we pulled into the lighted garage of my family's cape. Dinner was waiting. My dad asked me how my day was. That's how it always was.

That night I realized the lessons were mine.

## ANALYSIS

This essay is successful because it deals with a topic that is the subject of a plethora of essays every year and puts a unique and deeply personal spin on it, allowing it to stand out in the mind of its reader. The first half of the essay follows a familiar tune, as an ostensibly privileged high school student volunteers to help a neglected youth at the Boys' and Girls' Club. Our narrator struggles to reach the boy, but alas the breakthrough happens and the boy completes a long-division problem on his own. This section firmly establishes the narrator as an experienced teacher and the youth as a struggling pupil, making the twist at the end all the more effective.

Rhetorically, the essay is not stagnant; the author limits the narration of events to a bare minimum, stressing instead the relationship between himself and the boy. Nor, as the essay reaches its climax and the young boy patters up behind him, does he waste paper on an inevitably trite passage explaining his feelings. This is a remarkably effective device for two reasons. First, such a passage is unnecessary because the reader realizes that the power of the situation is such that it cannot be captured by words like "sad" or "bewildered"; and second, by not dictating to the reader how he felt, he allows the reader to put himself or herself in the author's place and read his or her own feelings into the essay.

The essay could profit, however, from more detail. It ends abruptly, and the writer fails to detail what these "lessons" actually are. The writer could improve his essay by including more details about how this anecdote affected him personally—and not just the way he behaved in a tricky situation.

Still, in showing that it was he who was the naïve pupil, the author takes on the role of teacher vis-à-vis the reader. He teaches by showing the reader how he or she would feel in a comparable situation, and establishes himself as a person with valuable experience to teach not only to the reader but also, crucially, to his fellow students in the next admitted class.

—William C. Marra

# "E Pluribus Unum"

By Corey Rennell, who attended a public high school in Anchorage, Alaska.

Armed men towered in military camouflage, bearing shields, helmets, bulletproof vests, steel-toed boots, and fireproof gloves, gripping aggressive black machine guns, pepper spray bottles, and tear-gas canisters.

*I had finally made it. I was finally united with the company of more than 60,000 international comrades, the moment I had longed for, the message I had risked everything to portray. Here we were in principle to protest the Summit of the Americas and no one could take us down, we could never be turned away. My parents were wrong. I was right to run away. Had I knowingly ignored the consequences of the Free Trade Area of Americas agreement I would never have been able to forgive myself.*

With undetected stealth, suddenly helicopters deafeningly pulsating not 50 meters above me as war machines filed in on all sides. Without warning, I was enveloped into the core of a furious crowd, too quickly to restrain; attacked from all directions with chemical nerve gas in burning canisters launched from rapid-fire armored tanks, sprayed with colossal water cannons, pelted with bruising rubber bullets, and surrounded by armed officials.

*And there was pain. And there was more pain. And there was crying. And there were tears. My tears. And there was only the bleeding cement to hear me. Only the torn and toppled fence to shield me from Them. Only the broken shop windows to keep It all away. I was Alone.*

The air thickened with a venomous texture, as my eyes burned and my throat stung as if it was being wrenched from my body. My pores screamed out for relief, inadvertently absorbing the lacerating agents of pain that had encased me as I frantically jabbed at my eyes trying to wipe it away.

*What I experienced was the most brutal, frightening, and painful journey of my lifetime. I had traveled 4000 miles, 16 hours on dark highways, 8 hours on stuffy trains, and was left with a hole the size of $1200 dollars in my pocket; all to publicly aggravate 8,000 police officers. Quite the ridiculous aspiration for a fifteen-year-old. Not only was I risking being arrested and detained in a foreign prison and potential sporadic police brutality just witnessed at the WTO protests in Seattle, I was risking my post-secondary plans that an arrest record would surely challenge. All to be assaulted in Canada.*

But beneath the voracious beating of helicopter propellers, amidst the gunfire-perpetrated colored fog, and above the silent fall of pain-inflicted tears I stood, surrounded by more than 50,000 individuals all uniting no matter their differences under one message for a cause circumnavigating the globe. Chanting for one purpose, one injustice in dozens of languages. All leaving their quarrels, religious conflictions, and warring cultures behind. We were all risking everything, together.

## ANALYSIS

The author tries something very difficult with this essay and comes away with mixed results. He attempts to narrate an experience on two levels—first, at the level of events he took part in, and second, at the level of his "emotions" during those events. In any essay, but particularly one such as this, which relies so heavily on clarity, language, and diction should be as perfect as possible. But the author misses several grammatical errors that slow the flow of the account and hinder its effectiveness. For example, both sentences of the third paragraph contain errors that make it seem convoluted and difficult to understand. The reader finds himself going over the paragraph twice to ascertain its full meaning.

The author shows creativity in telling the story on two levels, but he does not maintain an effective separation between the "action" and "emotion" parts of his essay. For example, is what distinguishes the third and fifth paragraphs from the fourth that the former are italicized and the latter is not? They all speak of the author's feelings. Indeed, the fourth paragraph, ostensibly the "emotions" paragraph, speaks the least to the author's actual "emotions." Perhaps a better technique would have been to narrate the nonitalicized parts in the third-person and the italicized parts in the first-person to better differentiate the parts.

The essay, however, is not without its merits. The account establishes the author as a person who strongly believes in his cause and is willing to stand up for perceived injustices in the world. While you might not have as sensational a story, an account of standing up for something you believe in is a particularly effective essay topic. Meanwhile, juxtaposing events you took part in with your emotions during those events can also be a successful way to tell your narrative.

—William C. Marra

# MOLDING IDENTITY

# "Religion Reconsidered"

By Alexis Maule, who attended a small private high school in Chicago, Illinois.

I had never questioned religion. My father was raised an Episcopalian altar boy and my Colombian mother, a Catholic, only stepped into church for special occasions. In both cases, however, challenging Jesus or "Papa Dios" was as blasphemous as committing murder, even though they couldn't come up for a reason why. The "why" question led me to reconsider my religious beliefs.

After nine years of attending church I had one message drilled into my tiny head: if you were good and prayed to God, He would help you when you needed Him. I remember my first cry for help as if it was yesterday. I made a sanctuary with candles at the foot of my ill father's bed. I got down on one knee and prayed like I had never prayed before. I pleaded with God to save him. To watch over him. To cure him. The next day I awoke feeling lively because I knew our family would be restored. That same day my father died, and my nine-year-old world came to a stop. I started researching the why of everything, especially religion. My father was one of the most pious men anyone knew. After my father died I hated God. He did not exist to me.

When I was thirteen it came time for Confirmation. I spoke to my deacon about religion before the ceremony because I wasn't sure I wanted to commit myself to the Episcopalian church. Over lunch I asked her tons of questions. How do people talk to God? Why do we worship a work that is sexist and contradicts scientific evidence? The questions that I had when I came into her house remained unanswered when I came out. The only thing she could say is to have faith. As a result, I was never confirmed.

Two years later I took the course European History A.P. and we began to read about the Enlightenment. I felt a great sense of resolution reading everything I had felt about religion scripted eloquently by Nietzsche when I read the works and his claim that religion was for the weak. I picked up Freud on my own and just consumed every word he wrote about religion.

I compare the Bible to the D'Aulieres book of Greek myths—there may be lessons to learn and lively characters to study, but it is more of an imaginative attempt to explain creation. I believe that how I do as a person is not dictated by a God. Essentially, people are in charge of their destinies. I have learned the hard way that society is not accepting of these beliefs. Even the closest people in my life reject my lack of religious beliefs. However, I am comfortable with myself and am fortunate to have gone on my very own unique religious journey. The biggest lesson I have learned from my religious journey is to never let anyone mold my beliefs. On any topic I must listen, investigate and form my own beliefs rather than follow the status quo.

## ANALYSIS

At a sparse five hundred words, admissions essays are often sorely lacking the fundamentals of quality writing—narrative detail, character development, even plot. But Alexis manages to include all those elements and then some in an essay which stays within the tight word count yet never feels hurried or deficient.

Clearly, Alexis's essay is focused on her philosophical development with respect to religion. But as she takes us across a span of roughly ten years in just a few minutes of reading, we also learn a surprising amount about her background. Alexis tell us her mother is Colombian, but she tells us even more in two quick words, "Papa Dios," a phrase which brings us right into her home as we imagine a childhood dominated by a cultural, not just religious, deity.

Similarly, when Alexis describes kneeling at her father's bedside, her writing adopts a genuinely prayerful tone. "I pleaded with God to save him," she writes. "To watch over him. To cure him." Those sentence fragments might annoy a middle school English teacher, but they're perfect for this essay. A daughter pleading for her father's life is, of course, permitted to speak in fragments, and Alexis's use of them here adds a powerful sense of authenticity.

Professing one's atheism in an essay like this could be considered a risk; after all, who knows what the religious sensibilities of your admissions officer might be? But Alexis's strong will is part of her point, and the background she provides suitably justifies whatever conclusions she might draw. And in any event, while the topic here is God, the essay is more fundamentally about Alexis's curiosity and academic spirit. She is demonstrating her ability to question and process her knowledge.

The essay could benefit from some polishing, especially in the third paragraph, where some verb tenses are inconsistent. And proofreading is always important: in the draft she submitted, "Confirmation" was not capitalized, and "Nietzche" was spelled incorrectly.

But Alexis has still constructed a remarkable essay which packs a great deal of information about her into such a maddeningly small space. And her conclusion—"I must listen, investigate and form my own beliefs"—is an unbeatable pitch for admission to any school that values independent thinking.

—Zachary M. Seward

# "A Periodical Affair"

By Karen Feng, who attended a small public school in New York City.

My love affair with *The New York Times* began two years ago. I had had minor trysts with several other newspapers, including a summer-long attachment to the Garfield comics and Cryptoquotes of *Newsday*, but the *Times* was the first paper I made a serious commitment to with a home delivery subscription. I entered into the relationship timidly at first, choosing to receive the paper just five days a week, but last year I took it one step further by ordering the weekend editions as well. I became deeply involved with the *Times*; I was enjoying every moment of it, and I still am.

I make time for my beloved newspaper whenever I can. When I come home on a typical weekday afternoon I get myself into some comfortable clothes, have an orange or some Cheerios, and sprawl down on the carpet of my living room with the day's *Times*. I explore the myriad sections one by one, spreading each one out to its full, expansive size, and take in the distinctive scent of fresh, clean newsprint. The tidy, hardcover-worthy text is a comfort to my eyes, and I scan the magnificently written stories with ease. After an hour or so of perusing I grudgingly pull myself away for a less exciting activity and carefully fold the sections back into place with a sigh. When I'm busy or on the run, I sift out a few sections and bring them to the train or to my room. I don't have the convenience or the pleasure of opening the pages to their full size in the crowdedness of a subway car or my desk, but the opportunity to read and absorb them well outweighs the trouble.

What I like most about *The New York Times* is that it is consistently abounding in interesting and informative articles. When I first encountered the paper I was slightly put off by the lack of a comics page, but I soon found that it had much more to offer me than a few cheap laughs. Every day it presents me with pieces exploring a wide variety of topics that extend far beyond the standard fare of national news, sports, and business. I have read and learned about such unusual subjects as gold panning in Siberia, the development of rooftop parks in Tokyo, the growth of the graphic novel industry, and, one of my favorites, the production process of a Steinway piano. I especially enjoy reading accounts of trends and daily life from various locales around the world. In addition, some of the specialized sections like Thursday's Circuits and House & Home pages have wormed their way into my weekly reading schedule and have deepened my enthusiasm for those subjects. If I am not satisfied with the day's main offerings, I can still make thorough use of the paper by finding something of interest in the depths of an overlooked section like World Business. Rare is the instance when I have come away from the *Times* not feeling enriched, fulfilled, or amused.

I have grown fonder of the *Times* as I read more. I began to keep a notebook of articles, photos, and recipes I clipped from the paper. I wrote to them a couple of times and one of my letters was published. At one point my attitude bordered on the edge of fanaticism, as I was reading little besides the paper each day. I insisted that *The New York Times Magazine* was the best glossy out there, and ditched *TIME*, my weekly companion of several years, for it. Since then, my passion has cooled down a good deal and I have readmitted other periodicals into my life. But my heart still races in anticipation every morning when I meet my dear newspaper on the front porch, as I await all the fascinating news, fit to print, that the *Times* will deliver.

## ANALYSIS

This admissions essay is very promising. It makes the reader feel like they know the author, it uses a variety of syntax and vocabulary, and it is well broken up, making it an easy read for any admissions officer. The author clearly dodges the pitfalls of publishing the whole thing in one or two monster paragraphs and seeming redundant. The frequent use of very simple constructions in the first two paragraphs, all beginning with "I + (verb)," make the reader feel as if they are listening to the essay firsthand and actually talking to the author. This technique is a quick and concise method of fleshing out the narrator—something that is important in an essay limited to approximately five hundred words. The author keeps the repeated use of the same structure interesting by breaking it up with interesting punctuation such as a semicolon and two hyphenated and creative adjectives.

The topic, the author's evolving relationship with *The New York Times*, is interesting taken at face value, but also serves the symbolic purpose of illustrating the author's transformation from a child to a young adult. We trace her evolution from Garfield comics and Cryptoquotes to a hard-core dedication to a paper which publishes an enormous volume of hard-hitting news daily while devoid of any comics. She effectively demonstrates that she has matured and is a young adult ready to enter a competitive Ivy League university.

The author uses very good examples to illustrate her point. The naming of specific sections of interests such as the Circuits pages, which aren't very well known, illustrate that either she really does read the *Times* every day thoroughly, or has done a bit of research on the topic.

While the topic serves its purpose well, it is a little cliché. Attempting to show that you are intelligent is not necessary in a college essay—that's what the transcript and standardized test scores are for. Most students applying to Harvard have an interest in what's going on in the world and writing about subscribing to *The New York Times* doesn't really differentiate this author from the twenty thousand other applicants. Furthermore, while the *Times* is an impressive publication, the news it presents is not dramatically different from the news presented in other major papers in the country. The author never describes why she chose the *Times* as the object of worship instead of *The Washington Post*, *The Wall Street Journal*, or *The Boston Globe*. A few sentences explaining why the author is obsessed with print media, and why that obsession has been focused on the *Times*, could have cleared up this problem.

—Joshua P. Rogers

# "The Art of Penning"

By Lan Zhou, who attended a large public school in San Diego, California.

Bernstein had his baton, Connors had his racquet, and I . . . I have my pen. True, I know that a pen's main purpose is to "communicate ideas via paper," but to me, it is more than writing utensil. A pen is the integral tool for the undiscovered art of penning—the long cylindrical writing instrument is the key to my passion of pen twirling.

My first experiences with penning started on my trips home in traffic. Every afternoon, my bored fingers wandered around the car: opening compartments, exploring niches, searching for something, anything, interesting to end the mundane ride. One day, I laid my hands on an old chewed-up pen jammed under my seat. With the radio stuck on country, the traffic crawling at two feet per minute, and my dad too exhausted for conversation, I resolved to entertain myself with the ratty old pen.

My first attempts to toss and catch the pen evoked worried cries about blinding my eyes in a moving car, so I proceeded to flip the pen through my fingers. As I continued to toy with the pen, I stumbled upon a new delight—my pen twirling lifestyle.

As I gradually learned, spinning a pen is an aesthetic art form requiring dexterous fingers and deep concentration. To refine my pen twirling skills, I detailed a weekly exercise routine for my ten little phalanges. During the car rides home, my fingers warmed up with armrest splits, practiced with dashboard push-ups, and cooled off with window waves. But as a true master of art, I know that strength alone is futile; precise timing and rhythm are essential to the perfect execution of a pen rotation. So, to enhance the artistic aspect of my penning, I twirled to music and spun to beats. Eventually, my phalanges mastered intricate backwards pinky twirls and thumb sommersaults; after countless hours in traffic, I had whipped my ten stubbly fingers into performing acrobats.

While some people can wiggle their ears and others can fold their tongues, I can twirl a pen. Even though I still use the pen to write essays, take notes, and fill out college applications, the pen has taken an additional role in my life. But until I can represent the US in pen twirling at the 2008 Olympics or start a pen-twirling craze at Harvard, only my friends and I will know of my hidden art. For me pen twirling is a knack, a talent, and a joy.

## ANALYSIS

Not every applicant can emulate this author's rhythmic prose, but "The Art of Penning" adheres to three rules from which all applicants can learn. First, the author exhibits a broad but not pretentious vocabulary. Admissions officers shouldn't ever have to consult a dictionary to understand an essay. Second, the author uses allusion effectively and not excessively. Conductor Leonard Bernstein and tennis star Jimmy Connors are both sufficiently common names that most readers will recognize the essay's opening analogy. It's important not to distract the reader by referencing little-known literary works or obscure historical events. Third, the essay stays focused on a single topic. The author includes no superfluous details; his brevity shows that he respects the extraordinary time pressures that admissions officers face.

Finally, and most importantly, "The Art of Penning" offers a hilariously sarcastic parody of the college admissions essay. The author follows the standard sequence of choosing a challenge, practicing with perseverance, and seeing the effort through to success. Yet the challenge is so absurd that readers can't help but smile at the sheer silliness of the subject. The careful choice of title, however, shows that the author appreciates this absurdity. "Penning" appears to have a clever double meaning. The author only superficially writes about the talent of twirling; beneath the surface, he offers a primer in the art of penning an admissions essay.

—Daniel J. Hemel

# "Myung!"

By Myung! H. Joh, who attended a large public school in Marietta, Georgia.

*The hot-blooded Spaniard seems to be revealed in the passion and urgency*
*of his doubled exclamation points . . .*
— Pico Iyer, "In Praise of the Humble Comma"

A re you a member of the Kung! tribe?" is a commonly asked question when people see my signature, which has an exclamation point at the end of it. No, I am not a member of any tribe, nor am I putting the mark at the end of my name to be "cute." It is not simply a hiccup in my handwriting; it is there for a specific reason. But before I elaborate on why I believe the exclamation point is such an appropriate punctuation mark for me, let us explore the other marks I might have used:

Myung?

Although the question mark bears a certain swan-like elegance in its uncertain curves, it simply does not do the job. While it is true that I am constantly discovering new things about myself and changing all the time, I know what I stand for, what my weaknesses and strengths are, and what I would like to get out of life. I know that I want to major in English, attend graduate school, learn as much as possible from those who are wiser than I, and eventually teach at a university. I am headed for a career in English; there is no question about it.

Myung,

I admit that I do pause and contemplate decisions before leaping in and rushing ahead of myself—spontaneity is perhaps not my strong point. But the comma, with its dragging, drooping tail, does not adequately describe who I am, because I know that life will not pause for me; nor do I want it to. Amid the chaos of a hectic schedule that balances clubs, activities, and AP courses, I always feel the rush of life, and I love it. I do not linger over failures; due to my passionate nature, I am crushed by disappointments, but I move on. No prolonged hesitations or pauses.

Myung:

I constantly look forward to the surprises that college and my future life promise me; graduation seems like the beginning of a whole new chapter. But the colon, though I will not deny its two neat specks a certain professional air, does not do me justice. I know how to live for today, have fun, and enjoy life instead of just waiting for what the next chapter may bring. The future is unpredictable. My present life is not simply the precursor to what may follow.

Myung.

Perhaps this is the most inaccurate punctuation mark to describe who I am. The drab, single eye of the period looks upon an end, a full stop—but with the greater aspects of my education still ahead of me, me life is far from any kind of termination.

Myung!

However, the exclamation point, with its jaunty vertical slash underscored by a perky little dot, is a happy sort of mark, cheerful, full of spice. Its passions match mine: whether it be the passion that keeps me furiously attacking my keyboard at 4:50 in the morning so that I might perfectly capture a fantastic idea for a story, or the passion that lends itself to a nearly crazed state of mind in which I tackle pet projects of mine, such as clubs or activities I am especially devoted to.

One of my greatest passions, my passion for learning, engenders in me a passion for teaching that I plan to satisfy fully as a professor. I want my students to feel the aching beauty of John Keats's words, his drawn-out good-bye to life. I want them to feel the world of difference in Robert Frost's hushed "the woods are lovely, dark and deep," as opposed to his editor's irreverent "the woods are lovely, dark, and deep." I want them to feel the juiciness of Pablo Neruda's sensually ripe poetry when he describes the "wide fruit mouth" of his lover. With the help of my exclamation point, I want to teach people how to rip the poetry off the page and take it out of the classroom as well. I want them to feel poetry when they see the way the sharp, clean edges of a white house look against a black and rolling sky; I want them to feel it on the roller coaster as it surges forward, up, as the sky becomes the earth and the ground rushes up, trembling to meet them; I want them to feel it in the neon puddles that melt in the streets in front of smoky night clubs at midnight. I want them to know how to taste life!

My exclamation point symbolizes a general zeal for life that I want to share with others. And I know that it has become as much a part of me as it has my signature.

## ANALYSIS

This essay uses a small punctuation mark to make a big point, loudly and forcefully. It answers the question "Who are you?" in a notably creative, exciting, and elucidating manner. Through an unconventional presentation, the author manages to captivate the reader's attention, while informing him/her of substantially revealing personal qualities. The strong, energized voice that is used delivers both a general, palpable sense of enthusiasm and a glimpse into specific ways that it manifests in the author's life.

The technical writing in this essay demonstrates skill. Each paragraph expresses one idea with cogency and brevity. A personified punctuation mark is presented through an interesting image and is then related to in light of the author's character. The final lines of each paragraph then cleverly bring a close to the ideas presented therein.

Though the addition of an exclamation mark could be seen as gimmicky, the author demonstrates that she has the energy and thoughtfulness needed to back up her unusual choice, in real life and on the page. It is obviously not a decision she has made lightly, nor just to make her application stand out, although one gets the impression that Myung! would stand out in any crowd, regardless of her name. It's a risky move, but for her, it works.

—Erin D. Leib

# "A Railroad of Memories"

By Masha Godina, who attended a large public school in Boulder, Colorado.

I perch on the upper bunk of my kupeh and observe Time as I ride the train of my childhood from Simferopoli (the capital of Crimea, Ukraine) to Moscow. It is a trip I have taken every summer for the first seven years of my life. I sit in the kupeh (sleeping compartment of the train) that has not changed in nine years, and I think of the implications. Visits like these form the different world in which I abide: the language I speak at home, the books I read, the family visits I take, the experiences, and, most of all, the memories I have.

I gaze down through the window at the railway tracks running backwards below. My thoughts run back in time, as if by analyzing my childhood and all of the places I have experienced will help me understand the Masha of the present. The reason I can shock others into laughter or understanding, the reason I think differently from my friends, is rooted in the confluence of drastically different philosophies of people with whom I have spent time. It is composed of the stops along memory lane, or "memory railroad" as is said in Russia. The railroad of my memory is framed by a blend of most varied scenery, for I have been submerged in most disparate philosophies: I have lived in the Soviet Union, in a conservative town in Canada, and in the ultra liberal granola-belt of Boulder, Colorado. I have grandparents who believe that Stalin is the best thing to happen to the world, and I distinctly remember the day I ceased to live in a Communist country. . . .

I am jerked out of my time travels by the train's sudden stop. "Hot pyrojky!" yells a voice outside my window. I am thrown back into the moment. Now, here, I am on this train. I am in Russia. I have Time. It is beautiful. I photograph the moment with my mind and carefully store it in my memory of things never to forget.

The window is curtained with a little blue cloth for aesthetic reasons and with a thick blue drape practical for blocking the sun's glare, casting delicious blue rays into the air already surfeited with the hot, rich aroma of food. The aroma renders the beauty tangible, and I know that this train is one of the places I can always return to for a taste of the lovely past.

My past forms who I am, for it shapes what I can share: the past and days like today, snippets of the present, form the inner world that I love so much, yet which is so inaccessible to others. Still, much as I love this world of memories, I cannot remain here for long. I'm not a private person. I believe that the best cure for any problem is talking about it. I cherish interaction. Experiencing these realities fills me with so much emotion that I run the risk of eruption. I want to share it, to bring pieces of it to everyone! I am someone lucky enough to have been completely absorbed in two utterly different societies. I have moved enough times, visited for long enough periods, that I could submerge myself completely in each world, and I have had the time to combine these pure experiences into a blend unique only to me. The world I see through the polychromatic prism of my memories is so beautiful that I want everyone to partake, to taste the variety that life can hold.

And there I go again, into the world of musing in which I so love to linger, visiting the American world in my thoughts, while I am very much in the Russian one. This moment is more than a future memory: it is the reality of today. It is the life. And it's bustling, for the train is teeming with energy. The kupeh door is half-closed, granting a glimpse of the raucous hall life: Mothers lovingly running up and down the narrow strip of communal space, shouting at their misbehaving children, the shabby carpet that constantly crumples. The conductor, an unwieldy lady in the never-changing white shirt and blue skirt, pokes her head in: "Are you a citizen of Russia or Ukraine?"

"Russia," I reply, smiling that the possibility of my being one of the handful of American passengers doesn't cross her mind. A temporary resident of the world where McDonald's is fondly known as "the international chain of free bathrooms," I laugh at ironies apparent only to me.

People passing by can't help but gawk—the curiosity of seeing others' activities is unbearable in the face of the tantalizingly unimpeded door. I love letting them see just my Russian life, developing the character I imagine I would have been had I stayed in Moscow. The game is propelled by necessity—we very well know that any mention of our current residence would leave us exposed to the much feared "tamojniky" (custom officers) searching for a bribe. And although I used to cry for the poor tamojniky whom everyone so disliked—not believing in "bad guys" even as a five-year-old—I now see the importance of divulging nothing extra. I heard the static-y conversation of their walkie talkies: "Hey, Iliuh, I've found a Russian, a Canadian, and two Americans in this kupeh," and the hearty reply: "well, Ha-appy Birthday!" And so I become the studious Russian schoolgirl emerging from my book or journal to chatter in a language that is fully my own, airing a vital piece of my reality into the sleepy room.

The bunk's subtle softness, the blue tint of light filtered through the curtains, the pounding of raindrops, and the gentle rocking and growling of the train are very conducive to sleeping, but the peace of the upper bunk also makes it an ideal place to read and write. The train ride gives me the gift of time and I refuse to waste it—nudged into a pure Russian world, I will think, analyze, and write as my past and my future merge into who I am, who I have become, now, here, observing Time on a top bunk of the train of my childhood.

## ANALYSIS

With a cursory read, this essay seems an excellent piece of work—well-written, descriptive, and personal, if a tad clichéd at moments. It is rife with vivid descriptive details, and its depiction of "Time" as a tangible entity embodied by Godina's familiar surroundings is both interesting and unexpected. But the essay is far too long, and it sets up a discussion of the writer's memories, and then meanders through descriptions of the train, ending without ever actually addressing those things that supposedly form the basis of her identity. The writer repeatedly refers to her childhood and her memories, but never actually describes much of what she is alluding to. Why does her background allow her to "shock others into laughter or understanding"? What is it about the world in her "polychromatic prism" that is so beautiful? What does the "variety that life can hold" consist of for her, and which parts are from each of the different phases of her life? The anecdote of the tamojniky, the most compelling action in the piece, successfully answers this question. It portrays the uniquely Russian approach that the writer, with her worldly perspective, takes. The essay also focuses well on the interaction between her past in Russia and her more recent experiences living in North America, but the writer should show the effect of the intersection of these experiences rather than simply informing us of it.

While the essay contains many details and carefully wrought descriptions, like the one of the window, it should have a stronger thesis or argument. The writer meanders through nostalgic commentary on her surroundings in the train, but never returns to actually describing the relationship between the train and her childhood memories, and her memories and her current identity. The essay loses momentum, but ultimately it succeeds because of its strong writing. Descriptive metaphors suggest the importance of memory and heritage—like the kupeh door, half-open and half-closed, representing the writer's feelings about her own dual heritage.

—Katherine A. Kaplan

# "Mosaic"

By Laure E. De Vulpillières of France, who attended a large suburban-
Paris school with a private American section.

**I** **see my life as a mosaic.** There are many glistening, colored
pieces shaping themselves into what will become the big picture of
my future life. Parts of that picture are already in place. My favorite
subjects have to do with language and culture, with history, politics
and international relations, with writing and public speaking, with environment and human rights.

**I love class discussions in English.** It is such fun to ponder every
word and debate its meaning. I love the sense of "oh, wow!" after finding a link, a theme or a symbol in a passage. My eyes get a little wider.
When I excitedly tell the class of my discovery, we all enthusiastically
scribble my idea into the margin of our texts. Their input excites me,
too. One girl will share her insight; the boy next to me will give another
dimension to that thought and then the intellectual, quiet girl in the
back row will reluctantly suggest her idea, which breaks the complex
phrase right open . . . and then we all think, "oh wow!"

**Our French class last year was just as interesting.** Our
teacher had us read over thirty literary texts of about 20 lines each.
Her perceptiveness was amazing! For each text, she would identify
three to five themes which she discussed up to four hours. At first, I
was overwhelmed by the richness and variety of her insights and had
trouble keeping up. Later, though, I was able to recognize those themes
even before we started the discussions, analyzing the intricacies and
appreciating the care that the authors put into crafting phrases.

**I've had five years of Spanish,** but I really fell in love with the
language and culture during my four trips to Spain. Like Americans,
the Spanish are open and welcoming to visitors. Like the French, the
Spanish have an incredible ancient culture of which they are not only

proud, but extremely knowledgeable. On a visit to Spain with my parents, a priest overheard us speaking French and came over to welcome us. Then he spent an entire day sharing the history and treasures of his village with us. His progressive religious beliefs, his warm sense of humor, his encyclopedic knowledge and his patient concern about our understanding his country presented Spain to us in ways that could never be learned in a classroom.

**I have always been fascinated by history.** I remember the disbelief that I first felt at the realization that so much had happened before I was even born. The Egyptians had built the pyramids, Tito had resisted the Soviets, Algeria had declared independence from France and it had all been done without my help. My childlike ego took a hard blow. However, I remain captivated by this past this is imposed upon us at birth. With a wealth of intricate detail, my history teachers have outlined significant events from all angles to help us understand each nation's strategies and hopes. They have taught me how our past shapes our minds, lifestyles, loyalties . . . and our future.

**I enjoy math, I really do . . .** once I understand it. I had some problems last year because my teacher was impatient when I asked questions. However, my teacher this year is encouraging. She says my level is good and she thinks I will get an A on the math section of the Baccalaureate. I am thrilled (and relieved)!

**One day I read a scientific news article** about gene technology and found I understood it, thanks to my class in biology. Until then, I had never realized how relevant my biology class is to me. Now I am fascinated and pleased that I can read a wide variety of scientific articles, especially when they have to do with my interest in the environment.

**Physics is not interesting to me.** As terrible as that sounds, I am not at all interested in calculating the speed of a ball that falls 3 meters to the ground or in estimating how many times it will bounce. Physics is too dry, too meticulous, and has nothing to do with people.

**Sit in any classroom almost any day of the year** and you will hear the sound of nose blowing, coughing and sneezing. The students at any school are not a healthy bunch. There is a good reason for that. Most focus only on academia, disdain their bodies, smoke regularly and hate to exercise. I have stopped telling people at school that I jog before school to keep in shape. They just don't understand why I think it's such a *great* way to start the day.

**For three years, I took judo and Chinese boxing.** I learned to focus my inner energy, to connect with my opponents' energy and to use this energy against them (for example, in upsetting their balance). Now, I often use this focusing technique when I want to convince someone of my ideas.

**During the entire week, I look forward** to our two hours of Model UN debates after school each Wednesday. I relish my transition from mere student to important world leader. It is all a simulation of course, but we Model UN-ers enjoy the seriousness of the debates, following protocol to the letter. On subjects of great importance to the future of international relations, we become true delegates, fighting for acceptance of our country's point of view.

**Five years ago, my older brother** started me thinking about environmental protection when he quoted scary examples of environmental destruction. Eager to spread my new knowledge, I was happy to see a sign announcing a new Ecology Club. However, at the first meeting, I found that the organizing teacher and I were the only ones there. We were both disappointed no one else had come, but we talked about recruiting other people and organizing activities. One week later, my efforts had brought in twelve participants. Since then, countless volunteers have helped organize events, raise money and spread the word about how each of us can protect the environment.

**Last summer, at the National Young Leaders Conference** in Washington, D.C., I and 350 other enthusiastic students spent two weeks listening to famous speakers, participating in simulations of Congress and the Supreme Court and learning about the U.S. government. On Capitol Hill, I met a government teacher from California who was interning for his congressman. Learning I was from France, he offered to show me around. For three hours, he plunged into a fascinating explanation of the human side of Congress. For example, after emphasizing how the animosity between political parties slows the democratic process, he expressed excitement because, for the first time in a long time, Republicans and Democrats had worked together on a bill to balance the budget. I felt right at home because the politics reminded me of Model UN.

**I often feel compelled to write about horrendous events** that are not well-covered in the media. It really bothers me that unsuspecting readers might believe that the subjects in the news are the only important ones. For example, I am shocked that, until recently, the horrifying famine in North Korea had received so little attention or that few know about the oppression of women in Afghanistan who are not even allowed to see a doctor when they are ill. In *Crosscurrents*, we cover issues such as these in the hope that a well-informed student body will eventually spread the news to larger groups, if not to the entire world.

**In theater, I love acting like someone I'm not.** Paradoxically, it helps me learn more about myself. I believe that each character in a play represents a different side of us: the romantic, the heroic, the tragic, the haughty, the jester, the innocent. We may have repressed these traits in ourselves, but acting demands that we express them freely—no matter how stereotypical, complex, sad or ecstatic the character is. We must first identify these same emotions within ourselves and then express them convincingly so that the audience can empathize with our character. When I act, I have the impression that my character's emotions have been thrust into my body, allowing me to experience feelings that I've never known in real life.

**As a volunteer at our local animal shelter,** I look forward to sharing my time with lonely dogs. I choose four or five dogs to take on a long walk through the forest. I teach them to recognize their names, come, sit, and lie down. If I have time, I brush their coats: I really want them to look their best so that they will get adopted. I hope they are a little happier because of my small contribution.

## ANALYSIS

De Vulpillières's technique in "Mosaic" is to break her life down into its many pieces and to show the different facets of her personality, her myriad interests, and what is important and even not so important to her. "Mosaic" does an excellent job of painting a detailed picture of De Vulpillières and examining all her different sides. As this is an additional essay, the extended-list format works quite well, even though it is an unconventional and possibly risky approach. Because of De Vulpillières's exceptional writing ability and her fascinating life, this essay is very unique and truly excellent. However, a list format for a main essay might be precarious, and should most likely be reserved for supplementary essays. De Vulpillières's primary essay was about her experience at The Hague International Model United Nations.

The main strength of "Mosaic" lies in the fact that it is so eloquently written, particularly considering that De Vulpillières is an international student from France. She also lets her sense of humor peek through in several occasions, such as in her paragraph entitled "I enjoy math, I really do . . ." One of the most striking aspects of De Vulpillières's essay is her intellectual curiosity and ability. Her paragraphs about her fondness for history, class discussions held in English, and her trips to Spain reflect her love of learning and of constantly challenging herself. De Vulpillières is also courageous enough to comment on many things that she does not like, such as physics, and what she is determined to change, such as the media's lack of coverage of many "horrendous" world events. One particularly outstanding paragraph is the one in which she explains her reasons for loving acting in theater productions. Her life, from this essay, is truly fascinating and lively, showing to the reader her many passions—for the environment, stray animals, Model United Nations and politics, exercise and good health, acting, etc. "Mosaic" shows us who De Vulpillières is, and that she deeply cares about many important issues.

The only true weakness in this essay is that it occasionally becomes self-righteous. The paragraph about exercising seems slightly judgmental of her fellow students: "I have stopped telling people at school that I jog before school to keep in shape. They just don't understand why I think it's such a *great* way to get in shape." Despite that one minor shortcoming, "Mosaic" is a superbly well-written essay, extremely interesting, and, unlike most college essays, gives the reader a deep insight into who De Vulpillières truly is, what she cares about, and impresses us with her worldliness, enthusiasm, and intelligence.

—Marcelline Block

# "Myself"

By Jamie Smith, who attended a small private high school in Houston, Texas.

*A teenage girl, JAMIE, walks out on stage alone from stage left. She has brown hair that falls to her shoulders and deep blue eyes. She is wearing a white blouse and blue jeans and in her right hand is a pair of binoculars. The stage is dark except for a single spotlight following JAMIE across the stage. When she reaches the center, she sits down on the edge of the stage, her feet dangling over, and raises the binoculars to her eyes. She proceeds to stare at the audience through them for a few seconds, then slowly moves them away from her face.*

JAMIE: With these binoculars I can see each one of you on an extremely personal level. *(She brings the binoculars to her eyes then down again.)* Do any of you audience members by any chance have your own pair handy? *(scanning the audience)* I was afraid of this. Well, here, why don't you take mine for a while? *(She jumps off the front of the stage, hands a front row audience member her pair of binoculars, then resumes her previous position.)* Now look through those and tell me what you see. Be honest now, I could use a good session of constructive criticism. Wait, maybe if I stand up you could get a better look at my true self. *(She stands and gracefully turns around.)* Make sure you get every angle now. Okay, now tell me everything you know about me . . . not much to tell, is there. I mean, you really don't know what kind of person is standing up on this stage in front of you blabbering on about binoculars and constructive criticism. Well, I guess I have my work cut out for me today; I must describe who I am. Fortunately, I did come prepared. I have provided myself with a prop—and the influence of a very special person—to assist me throughout one of the most difficult performances of my life, an interpretation of a piece I call "Myself." *(She steps off the stage and returns to the audience member in the front row.)* Do you mind if I take these back now? *(She returns to the stage.)* The one prop is, you guessed it, a pair of binoculars.

Not just any binoculars, they are one of the few reminders I have of my great-grandmother, Gran. No, she wasn't an infamous spy at large during World War II nor was she an avid birdwatcher. In 1986, when I was six and she was ninety-four we both watched Halley's Comet make its celestial appearance through these binoculars. I remember she said that she and I were truly blessed because we both were able to see Halley's Comet twice in our lives. She told me about seeing it out in her backyard in 1909, when she was the same age I am now. There we were together, seventy-seven years later, watching the same comet shoot across the same sky. I think of all the things that have happened during those seventy-seven years, the triumphs and setbacks Gran achieved and endured, and it has given me strength to deal with the challenges in my own life. I imagine how much life had changed since 1909 and wonder how my life will change by the time I see Halley's Comet again. What will I become? I will not, like Gran, be a part of the Oklahoma land run or witness the birth of the automobile. I will probably not be quarantined for tuberculosis or listen to the progression of two world wars over the radio. But I know I will do and be something. And the determination and success of my great-grandmother will help me reach this something. She is more than a memory or a story, she has become a part of me: my family, my history, my source of knowledge and my source of pride. Her struggles and achievements are reflected in mine. She is with me when I rise and fall and always there to make sure my feet are still on the ground. She is with me backstage and with me in the spotlight. She is a woman. She is my great-grandmother. And that's truly what she is—great, grand, everything. Gran. It's amazing how a simple name can inspire so much.

*She sits down, returning to her initial position with her feet dangling over the edge. She brings the binoculars to her eyes and looks through them. But instead of looking at the audience, she is attempting to look beyond them, almost as if there is some invisible sky behind the rows of seats. She slowly moves the binoculars away from her face, but her eyes are still fixed on some object off in the distance.*

JAMIE: Only sixty-six years to go. I've got to make them count.

## ANALYSIS

Written in the format of a play script monologue, both in style and overall structure, this essay addresses the concept that it is difficult to evaluate a person from strictly superficial appearances. In order to truly know someone, no matter how closely you study their outer appearance, it is what's inside that counts. Emotions, thoughts, dreams, and personal goals are the most important and telling aspects of one's identity. The writer does not just theorize about such ideas, but makes a logical progression by giving a concrete, vivid example to back up her thesis. Without having to explicitly list interests or personality traits, the style of the essay reveals a good deal about the applicant: she probably enjoys acting or playwriting and is highly creative and optimistic about life.

One of the strongest aspects of the essay is the fact that it is written as a monologue. The creative format is going to stand out from the thousands of other application essays that admissions officers must read. The use of binoculars as a linking device between the present and the past is highly effective—it produces an overall coherence within the essay. The applicant's use of a very specific moment to frame her love for "Gran" increases the naturalness of the passage. In many cases, essays written about a family member can sound contrived. The use of a specific event adds to the realism of the applicant's emotion. The creative use of stage directions addresses the adage "show—not tell" head-on. It is an effective way of creating a mental picture of the applicant in a reader's mind. The essay also ends strongly as the last line clearly identifies that the applicant is ambitious, hard-working, and eager to make something out of her life.

The monologue of the essay is effective, but it is important to point out that such attempts to be overly creative can backfire. This applicant's familiarity with this style of writing is apparent. If you attempt to write your essay in a nonstandard manner, make sure you have a similar comfort level with the techniques you are using.

—Joshua H. Simon

# "Who Am I?"

By Michael Cho, who attended a small all-male suburban high school outside of Cleveland, Ohio.

I wish I could write about the Michael Cho who stars in my Walter Mitty-like fantasies. If only my personal statement could consist of my name followed by such terms as Olympic athlete, master chef, boy genius, universal best friend, and Prince Charming to every hopeful woman. These claims would be, at worst, outright lies, or at best, gross hyperbole. My dreams, however, take their place alongside my memories, experiences, and genes in the palette that constitutes who I am.

Who am I? I am a product of my reality and my imagination. I am innately depraved, yet I am made perfect. I plan my day with the knowledge that "Everything is meaningless" (Ecclesiastes 1:2), but I must "make the most of every opportunity" (Colossians 4:5). I search for simple answers, but find only complex questions.

Once, on my way to a wrestling tournament, I was so engulfed in thought over whether living in an abode which rotated near the speed of light would result in my being younger (utilizing the Theory of Relativity) and stronger (utilizing the properties of adaptation along with the definition of centripetal and gravitational force) that I failed to realize that I had left my wrestling shoes in my locker. My mother says that my decision to wrestle is indicative of the fact that I don't think.

Through working in a nursing home, the most important lesson I've learned is that I have many lessons yet to learn. Thus the most valuable knowledge I possess reminds me how little knowledge I have.

Oftentimes people make the mistake of assuming that mutually exclusive qualities bear no relationship to one another. Not so! These dichotomies continuously redefine each other. In some cases one is totally dependent on the other's existence. What is faith without doubt? Without one, the other does not exist. When juxtaposed, opposites create a dialectic utterly more profound and beautiful than its parts. Walt Whitman embraces this syncretism by stating, "Do I contradict myself? Very well then I contradict myself, (I am large, I contain multitudes)." My qualities, though contradictory, define who I am.

Although I can't make fantastic claims about myself, I must still acknowledge and cherish the dreams that I have. Admittedly, it is tragic when one is so absorbed in fantasy that he loses touch with reality. But it is equally tragic when one is so absorbed in reality that he loses the ability to dream. When a healthy amount of reality and fantasy are synthesized, the synergy is such that something beautiful will undoubtedly result.

## ANALYSIS

This applicant addresses the proverbial question of "Who Am I?" In doing so, he expresses, both implicitly and explicitly, his hobbies, extracurricular activities, and outlook on life. The writer not only reveals his participation in wrestling, work at a nursing home, and knowledge of Quantum Mechanics, but he also exposes the reader to many aspects of his personality and inner thoughts on life. His questioning of the meaning of life and evaluation of his own identity reveal an inquisitive side to his personality.

Overall, this essay is well written and easy to read. The introduction is strong in that the applicant levels with admission officer by admitting he does not consider himself to be a spectacular individual, giving the impression that what follows is written honestly. Another strong point of the essay is that it reveals many of the activities in which the writer is involved. This serves to give the admissions officer a more personalized picture of the applicant. The biblical and Walt Whitman quotations are very well used and demonstrate the strong intellect of the writer.

While the essay does provide some insight into the philosophical thoughts of the applicant, in many ways it is too theoretical. The writer

could improve the essay by specifically listing the dreams or goals he cher-
ishes or perhaps by writing in more detail about one of the many experiences he mentions in the statement. The flow of the essay is also hindered
in a number of ways. First, the word choice seems slightly unnatural—
almost as if the applicant relied on a thesaurus when writing the essay; as
a result, the tone seems to be a bit contrived. Second, while the overall
theme of self-identification is maintained throughout the essay, the individual paragraphs jump from one topic to the next in a disjointed fashion. For
example, it is interesting to know that the applicant worked at a nursing
home, but mentioning such does not seem to fit with the overall progression of the essay. It is important that the personal statement convey to the
admissions officer a sense of who you are and what you are like in person,
but it is not necessary to cram every extracurricular activity or accomplishment into the essay; there are other sections of the application for listing
such things.

—Joshua H. Simon

## "My Name"

By Uyen-Khanh Quang-Dang, who attended a public high school in Santa Clara, California.

W endy!"

I was walking down the hallway, my shoulders sagging from the weight of my backpack nearly bursting with books on the way to a student council meeting, from the worries of the canned food drive, from all the thoughts which cluttered my brain just moments before. I sank into a deep thought about the two names, Wendy and Uyen-Khanh.

My parents, my grandmother, and all my peers at the Sunday Vietnamese Language School knew me as Uyen-Khanh, my name as written on my birth certificate. Yet I was a wholly different person to my "American" friends and teachers—I had always been Wendy. Even some of the award certificates I received read: "Wendy Quang-Dang."

Wendy is an invented name bestowed upon me by my kindergarten teacher who decided that Uyen-Khanh was too difficult to pronounce. In fact, it became so convenient that I began to introduce myself as Wendy to avoid the hassle of having to slowly enunciate each syllable of "Uyen-Khanh" and hear it transformed into "won-ton" or "ooh-yen kong." It was especially hard on substitute teachers, who would look up from the roll book, flustered and perplexed as they tried their best not to completely destroy my name. Wendy also greatly decreased the looks of terror and embarrassment as people would struggle to remember how to say "Uyen-Khanh" two minutes after we had been introduced.

But at that moment standing alone in the hallway, I decided that I wanted to be known to all as one person: Uyen-Khanh. Wendy had served me well for the past eight years since kindergarten, but it was time I let go of a nickname and recognized the name written on my birth certificate.

It took me over three months of consistent persistence and patience to erase the name so many had known me by. Letting up on my determination to brand Uyen-Khanh into everyone's memory for even just a second was not a possibility if I wanted my mission to be successful. This meant pretending not to hear someone calling me unless it was some form of Uyen-Khanh. I would interrupt people mid-greeting and stand my ground when my friends would glare angrily at me and whine, "But I've always known you as Wendy!" My philosophy was that people must respect my wishes to say Uyen-Khanh. By the end of those three long months my resoluteness had paid off and I was richly rewarded by the sound of Uyen-Khanh pronounced smoothly and effortlessly by my closest friends.

I was thirteen years old born and raised in San Jose, the second largest Vietnamese populated city in the United States. A first-generation Vietnamese citizen of this country, English was as native to me as the language of my ancestors, Vietnamese. I grew up a "true American," as my grandmother would call it, for I did not just adapt to the all-American lifestyle, I lived it. When I decided to shed the name casually given to me in kindergarten, it seemed to some that I was "going back" to my true heritage, believing that being called Uyen-Khanh would somehow make me more Vietnamese. The truth was I was more "American" then ever when Uyen-Khanh replaced Wendy. Being born and raised in San Jose as a first-generation Vietnamese citizen made me who I am, a Vietnamese-American. Uyen-Khanh was just the name I was given at birth, and it was simply time to acknowledge it.

## ANALYSIS

Uyen-Khanh's essay falls squarely into the "identity" category, as the writer tells the story of defining her American identity by deciding to force her friends to call her by her given name, Uyen-Khanh, rather than a long-held American nickname, Wendy.

The writer expresses the difficulties she experiences and the persistence necessary to change the way she is viewed by her peers and teachers while stealthily squeezing in several allusions to her life as a busy student ("student council meetings," "Vietnamese Language School," and "canned food drives"). These allusions are so well integrated that her essay doesn't lose its flow or sense of direction, in fact, they show that she is very much the "true American" she says she is in the text.

This essay's greatest strength is in its style. Neither flowery nor over-written, the essay is simple and straightforward without being formulaic or trite. Uyen-Khanh efficiently tells the story of her name and links it to her identity as a Vietnamese American person at once deeply appreciative of her Vietnamese heritage and every bit an American. She does a good job of moderating her stance so that what could have been an angry treatise shows her to be firm and compassionate. It shows her to patiently refuse to yield when friends try to revert to her nickname, but at the same time al-lowing them time to get used to pronouncing her given name. Overall, this is a solid essay with good tone, pacing, and language.

There are few weaknesses to speak of in Uyen-Khanh's essay; if any-thing, she may have missed some opportunities to further expand on her description of herself as a Vietnamese American. Every college essay is a compromise of thoughts and space as one tries to strike a comfortable bal-ance between self-promotion and reflection. Ultimately, this essay reflects numerous good choices and results in a success.

—Jason M. Goins